The Education and Care of Children with Severe, Profound and Multiple Learning Difficulties

Richard Aird

Dedication

This book is dedicated to the staff, pupils and families of Baginton Fields School, Coventry, 1986–2000.

David Fulton Publishers Ltd
Ormond House, 26–27 Boswell Street, London WC1N 3JZ

www.fultonpublishers.co.uk

First published in Great Britain by David Fulton Publishers 2001

Note: The right of Richard Aird to be identified as the author of this work has been asserted by him in accordance with the Copyright, Designs and Patents Act 1988.

Copyright © Richard Aird 2001

British Library Cataloguing in Publication Data
A catalogue record for this book is available from the British Library.

ISBN 1–85346–708-1

Typeset by Book Production Services, London
Printed and bound in Great Britain by The Cromwell Press Ltd, Trowbridge, Wilts.

Contents

Preface

When I began work on this book, it was never my intention to produce a scholarly commentary upon the education and care of disabled children. My intention was always to provide a practical, common-sense approach to help meet the needs of a small group of pupils who probably present society with some of its greatest challenges. The fact that the bulk of the text was written on a personal computer perched on the edge of my family's kitchen table is, I believe, testimony of my intention to produce such a down-to-earth book.

However, on reading through the final draft, I am aware that the occasional critical comment found its way into the text. Despite my earlier good intentions, I have allowed these comments to stand within the published text. This is not because I believe I have produced a scholarly commentary by default. These comments remain because I feel that some measure of critical comment is becoming increasingly important for securing a meaningful future for the education and care of disabled children.

The management of a school for pupils with severe, profound and multiple learning difficulties is not an easy task. Neither is it an easy task for the staff who work in such schools to educate and care for their pupils as effectively as they might wish – or as others might wish. The changing world of child education has made the difficult job of educating and caring for disabled children significantly more difficult, and I do not apologise for making critical comment about things that I believe are proving to be damaging to the lives of these children and to the schools that cater for their needs.

Richard Aird
February 2001

Acknowledgements

In writing this book I am indebted to many people – in particular the professionals, parents and pupils whom I have worked alongside during my time as a head teacher and who have unselfishly shared their wisdom with me. I should also like to thank the first cohort of students on The Modular Course in the Education and Care of Children with Severe, Profound and Complex Learning Disabilities (Aird 2000c) for giving me the confidence to share my ideas, and Tina Tilstone of the University of Birmingham for prompting me to write them down. My special thanks go to my wife Karen, for her knowledge, assistance and unfailing encouragement.

CHAPTER 1

A recent history of rights, needs and deceptions

A question of entitlement

By the beginning of the new millennium, the United Kingdom's National Curriculum for education had been in operation for a decade or so and a wealth of material had been published about the relevance and implementation of that curriculum for pupils with severe learning difficulties (SLD) or profound and multiple learning difficulties (PMLD). Throughout the 1990s, enabling the rights of those pupils to access the National Curriculum had become something of a holy grail for academics and practitioners alike. The fact that the bulk of the National Curriculum was largely irrelevant and meaningless to the circumstances of many pupils with SLD/PMLD only seemed to excite further exploration and interest in discovering the key to the whereabouts of that holy grail.

Quite soon after the publication of the Education Reform Act 1988 (ERA88), the title of the newly published National Curriculum became synonymous and interchangeable with that of the more socially acceptable title of 'entitlement curriculum'. A common entitlement to the newly defined National Curriculum was presented as one of the cornerstones of ERA88 and in many ways ERA88 was seen as an Act that championed the right of all children to benefit from a minimum standard of educational opportunity. For many teachers it was the principle of entitlement that was felt to justify the imposition of the National Curriculum upon the special-school sector, regardless of the obvious shortcomings of that curriculum in terms of its relevance to pupils with special educational needs (SEN).

The design and content of the National Curriculum were not without some criticism, particularly in schools that specialised in the education of pupils with SLD/PMLD (SLD schools). This criticism was primarily because the starting point of the curriculum material tended to be pitched above the ability of many of their pupils and because the pace of learning was too great to allow for the relatively modest attainments of pupils with SLD/PMLD. However, SLD schools sought to implement the full National Curriculum, confident in their ability to modify the curriculum framework so as to make it more relevant to the abilities of their pupils. There were remarkably few pupils with SLD/PMLD disapplied from the National Curriculum, despite the provision of Section 18 of the ERA88, which allows pupils with SEN to be disapplied from all or parts of the National Curriculum in response to their individual circumstances. Head teachers of SLD schools took their collective stance upon the moral high ground that the principle of entitlement afforded and empowered the right of their pupils to benefit from access to the emerging broad and balanced National Curriculum.

During the early 1990s this ethical stance was reinforced by more pragmatic and mundane considerations. In addition to the provision of a National Curriculum, ERA88 also brought into being the Local Management of Schools (LMS) initiative. Rumour and conjecture was rife during the early 1990s with the belief that wholesale disapplication of the National Curriculum for pupils with SLD/PMLD might make the funding of SLD schools vulnerable and put the future of these types of school in doubt. This was a prospect that few SLD school head teachers were prepared to risk for the sake of criticising the quality of the National Curriculum.

Throughout the 1970s and 1980s, the prevailing ethos of SLD schools had been one that continued to advocate the rights of profoundly disabled children who, prior to the Education (Handicapped Children) Act 1970, had been denied access to a formal education. For many SLD practitioners, the National Curriculum was welcomed as representing another incremental step towards achieving the same social and legal rights for disabled children as those that were enjoyed by their non-disabled peers. The promise of an entitlement curriculum was regarded by the majority of SLD practitioners as something sacrosanct, and the benefits that would accrue to pupils with SLD/PMLD, as a consequence, were considered to be irrefutable. When teachers experienced difficulties in engaging pupils with SLD/PMLD in a meaningful way within the newly defined National Curriculum, attention was not focused upon the irrelevance of the curriculum material but rather upon ways in which teachers needed to make their pupils become active participants within it (Carpenter 1990).

Seeking ways to access pupils with SLD/PMLD to the National Curriculum became the preferred, politically correct way of lobbying for the rights of pupils with SLD/PMLD. There were few arguments advanced during the early 1990s that identified any need for a national strategy with which to establish common standards in the education, care and treatment of children with SLD/PMLD, despite the fact that the SLD sector had only been in existence for some two decades and was thus still in its infancy. The government had responded to calls for equality by developing a National Curriculum to which all school children had an equal entitlement, and the quality of education provided to all pupils – whether disabled or not – was to be determined by appraising the performance of pupils within the assessment framework of that curriculum.

With the demise of initial specialist teacher training in the mid-1980s, there had been a reducing pool of teachers who had a proper understanding about the aetiology and pedagogy of pupils with SLD/PMLD. It was unfortunate that, as the effect of this reduction in specially trained teachers began to bite in SLD schools, teachers were confronted by a National Curriculum that had little in common with the existing SLD curriculum they had inherited, and consequently teachers in SLD schools struggled to come to terms with the demands being imposed upon them. Despite brave words of advice from authors such as Sebba *et al.* (1995), implementation of the National Curriculum inevitably led to some dilution of the sound SLD curriculum practice that had been developed during the 1970s and 1980s. In addition, during that time many head teachers in SLD schools confused the task of empowering the rights of their pupils to access the entitlement curriculum with unwittingly allowing increased societal control of the way in which SLD schools functioned. Not all of these things were necessarily damaging, but undoubtedly they served to confuse SLD practice at the time and have continued to do so.

By 1997 some 34 per cent of teachers in SLD schools were reported as disagreeing that the National Curriculum offered a proper basis for a curriculum that was appropriate to the needs of their pupils (SCAA 1997b). Certain practitioners at that time declared that teachers in SLD schools were unknowingly participating in some kind of conspiracy of deception (Humphrey 1997) in their efforts to try to reconcile the teaching of the traditional SLD curriculum with the often alien subject-based material of the National Curriculum. Despite a growing sense of scepticism about whether it was possible to reduce subjects of the National Curriculum to levels that were relevant to the abilities of some pupils with SLD/PMLD (Turner 2000), the search continued unabated for identifying the means of allowing these pupils full access to their entitlement to the National Curriculum.

Seeking ways to make pupils with SLD/PMLD actively engage with the National Curriculum continued throughout the 1990s to be one of the primary concerns of authors who specialised in the education of these pupils. This preoccupation was despite authoritative advice that the National Curriculum was only intended to form part of the whole curriculum and that special schools should maintain a curriculum that was relevant to the needs of individual pupils (Dearing 1994; SCAA 1995; 1996a). The flood of advice about the various ways of differentiating how the National Curriculum could be used in SLD schools also continued, despite research findings indicating that the implementation of the National Curriculum had had minimal impact upon actual school practice (Halpin and Lewis 1996). This lack of impact was associated with the fact that teachers in SLD schools generally regarded the National Curriculum as being irrelevant to the needs of their pupils and/or only accepted its importance at the level of rhetoric (Marvin 1998). However, other forces were at work to ensure that the rhetoric of the National Curriculum would be taken seriously, regardless of its relevance to the needs of pupils with SLD/PMLD and regardless of the views that teachers in SLD schools had begun to voice.

The threat of failing school inspections being undertaken by agents of the Office for Standards in Education (OFSTED) during the 1990s no doubt encouraged the majority of SLD schools to fall into line and to continue to put the implementation of the National Curriculum at the top of their priority list. The threat of failing an OFSTED inspection was a powerful and motivating factor that worked to ensure the rhetoric of the National Curriculum could be seen to be implemented in full in the majority of SLD schools. Towards the end of the 1990s, the DfEE published findings from OFSTED inspections reporting that some 27 per cent of special schools had been found to have serious weaknesses or had been placed on special measures – a percentage that the DfEE advised was greater than those found in mainstream schools (DfEE 1998a).

Around the same time, some authors began highlighting the need for specialist curricula in response to specific disabilities. For instance, Powell and Jordan (1998) advised that the curriculum for children with Autistic Spectrum Disorder (ASD) should be based primarily upon individual pupil need rather than upon a National Curriculum that had been developed for non-disabled children. The cultural values relating to academic subjects of the National Curriculum were felt to be too far removed from the immediate needs of pupils with ASD to justify placing these subjects at the core of the special school curriculum. However, despite the fact that a growing number of pupils with ASD were being educated in SLD schools by the end of the 1990s, few SLD schools could be seen to be making the development of specialist curricula a matter of priority.

Many SLD schools opted instead to bolster their implementation of the National Curriculum and invested in curricula that had been developed with the intention of making the subject matter of the National Curriculum subjects at Level 1 more relevant to the needs of their pupils (e.g. the EQUALS baseline packs). No doubt the threat of failing a second, more robust, round of OFSTED inspections, organised from the late 1990s onwards, prompted SLD schools to place a higher priority upon implementation of the National Curriculum than they did upon developing specialist curricula in response to individual pupil need. Some authors described the teaching of the National Curriculum in SLD schools in this way as being no more than a façade of competence (Barber and Goldbart 1998) that had been designed to satisfy the demands of OFSTED but that had little in common with good SLD practice.

The idea of developing a Pre-Level 1 curriculum gained momentum towards the end of the 1990s and the title of 'P levels' became the preferred shorthand when referring to curriculum materials leading towards Level 1 of the National Curriculum. As more material was shifted from the traditional SLD curriculum into P level curricula, a curious hybrid of developmental/behaviourist/academic criteria emerged that was then presented by organisations such as EQUALS as a curriculum framework against which the assessment of pupil ability could be standardised. The relabelling of traditional SLD curricula in this way was contrary to advice at the time, which warned against the folly of this elaborate pretence (Byers 1999). Clinical practices were crudely clumped together with behaviourist strategies such as task analysis in the naïve belief that pupils with SLD/PMLD could be made to follow generalised patterns of development at a comparable rate of progress with pupils from other schools, regardless of the idiosyncratic disabling circumstances that the pupils were subject to. Seeking to incorporate traditional PMLD practice into the P level assessment framework was perhaps the greatest folly of the time. Pupils with profound and complex disabilities have for many years been known to be notoriously poor consumers of generalised curricula (Ware and Healey 1994) and recognised as requiring a curriculum that is based upon their individual need (SCAA 1996b). Moreover, the assessment of pupils with PMLD has been shown as requiring entirely different strategies than the conventional approach to assessment developed in respect to the National Curriculum (Barber and Goldbart 1998).

Despite what was known about the pedagogy of pupils with profound and complex disabilities, the first year of the new millennium was heralded by a consultation document commissioned by the Qualifications and Curriculum Authority (QCA)'s project entitled *Curriculum Guidelines for Pupils Attaining Significantly Below Age-Related Expectations* (Tilstone *et al.* 2000). Rather than seeking to define a discreet, tailor-made National Curriculum for pupils with SLD/PMLD, the emphasis of this major initiative was once again focused upon empowering pupils to access the National Curriculum by means of the jumble of developmental/behaviourist/ academic strategies that had become known as the P levels. The P level strategy was pursued by the QCA regardless of the findings published in *The P levels Project* (University of Durham 1999), which had demonstrated that, following trials of pre-Level-1 curricula, there had been a minimal impact on the raising of educational achievements reported for the majority of pupils with SLD and none at all for pupils with PMLD.

The belief that P levels were able to offer a framework for standardising the assessment of pupil ability within the whole curriculum was promoted from 1999 onwards, particularly by EQUALS, an organisation that encouraged individual SLD schools to compare the outcomes of their pupils' learning, in relation to the P levels, with those of other SLD schools across the country. This curious development did not appear to be prompted by the DfEE but grew out of the efforts of a small yet determined group of SLD head teachers. The use of P levels in this way sought to spite the proven shortcomings of P level curricula and its inherent assessment framework, and to spite also the government's advice that the National Curriculum was only ever intended to form part of the whole curriculum, with curriculum planning for pupils with PMLD needing to be directed by individual need rather than by adherence to subjects of the National Curriculum (SCAA 1996b).

During the year 2000, Lancashire Local Education Authority (LEA) went one step beyond the work of EQUALS with their grandly titled, *Performance Indicators for Value Added Target Setting* (PIVOT). The PIVOT package (Lancashire LEA 2000) extended the notional content of P levels, with the belief that pupil performance upon P level curricula may be used as *value-added* criteria for appraising the effectiveness of SLD schools on a national scale. Both EQUALS and PIVOT appear to have ignored the basic fact that the innate disabilities constraining the majority of children with SLD/PMLD dictates that they are unlikely to follow any generalised patterns of development (Brown *et al.* 1998). Attempts to impose hierarchical P level extensions onto the assessment framework of the National Curriculum in this way are inherently flawed. Teachers in SLD schools need to be aware that recent developments in the use of P levels may pave the way for information from pupil performance on P levels to be used to provide 'value-added' data influencing the teachers' performance-related pay. The possibility of such a development epitomises the worst form of societal control for governing the education, care and treatment of disabled children.

There have been, and will continue to be, benefits accruing to pupils with SLD/PMLD as a consequence of engaging them in subjects of the National Curriculum. Implementation of the National Curriculum in SLD schools led to a welcome broadening of the whole curriculum in these schools and to improvements in the manner in which pupils with SLD/PMLD were educated (Aird 2000a; Turner 2000). However, the design and content of the National Curriculum has not proved sufficient for providing a meaningful framework for defining good SLD practice on a national scale. Energy and resource that had been directed towards developing P level materials would have been far better directed towards developing a national strategy for guiding the development of the whole curriculum for pupils with SLD/PMLD. The P level initiative is not sufficiently relevant to the circumstances of severely disabled children as to be able to provide such a national strategy. As provision for pupils with SLD/PMLD progresses within the new millennium, it is not the development of P levels that should be given priority; instead, priority should be given to securing clarity of purpose for the whole SLD/PMLD sector, so that common sense may yet prevail.

Inclusion, value for money and accountability

Running alongside the implementation of the National Curriculum has been its stable mate from ERA88, the Local Management of Schools. The delegation of centrally held finances from LEAs direct to the governing bodies of schools was an essential component of government policy at the end of the 1980s and has remained so, despite changes in the complexion of government. The Education Act 1993 and the then Department of Education's Circular 2/94 (1994b) confirmed that LMS was to be fully implemented in the special-school sector (termed 'LMSS'). The section (276) that dealt with SEN issues in the Education Act 1993 was preceded and partly influenced in its construction by two important reports from the early 1990s jointly written by the Audit Commission and Her Majesty's Inspectorate of Education (HMI), namely *Getting in on the Act* (1992a) and *Getting the Act Together* (1992b). The common thread running through these reports, and the subsequent Act of Parliament, was concern about the lack of clarity that was felt to exist at that time regarding the definition of SEN and the manner in which pupils with SEN could have their education funded on an equitable basis (Aird and Bainbridge 1997).

Intrinsic to the matter of the joint Audit Commission and HMI reports was an emphasis upon the relative cost-effectiveness of integrating pupils with SEN into mainstream schools, as compared with maintaining them in relatively expensive special schools. Establishing value-for-money arguments for rationalised use of special schools provided a strongly motivating factor for some LEAs to place integration at the top of their priorities. It was significantly later that the DfEE sought to advocate (DfEE 1997) the educational and moral arguments for taking forward the integration (or 'inclusion', as it was termed in 1997) of pupils with SEN into mainstream education, thus demonstrating an unfortunate hierarchy of principles underpinning the dogma of inclusion during the 1990s.

LMSS became fully implemented in special schools by the mid-1990s, and the drive towards rationalising special schools continued with varying degrees of success in different parts of the country. Throughout the inclusion debate, there had been an enduring absence of any clear definition with which to govern the development of SEN provision. This was a shortcoming that an HMI Fish had commented on in the mid-1980s but that had been allowed to continue, despite the high profile of SEN in national strategy. Some ten years after the original observation made by HMI Fish (Fish 1985), the lack of clarity concerning the role of special schools and the nuisance of having under-developed methods for measuring special-school effectiveness were major findings in another report, *Enhancing School Improvement Through Inspection In Special Schools* (Sebba *et al.* 1996).

The drive towards developing an inclusive education system continued through the 1990s – regardless, however, of the fact that successive government strategies had failed to properly address known weaknesses in the SEN sector. In the publication entitled *A Review Of Special Schools, Secure Units and Pupil Referral Units In England* (OFSTED 1999), the authors concluded that special schools were becoming increasingly complex and alerted readers to the fact that SEN provision was failing to be developed along any unified national pattern. These were trends that had been known for many years but largely ignored by successive governments. The focus of attention remained upon the further development of the National Curriculum as a vehicle for securing an inclusive education system and for appraising the effectiveness of SEN provision.

The shortcomings of the National Curriculum have already been touched upon in the opening section to this chapter, and it may well be, sadly, that theories described as a 'conspiracy of deception' (Humphrey 1997) and a 'façade of competence' (Barber and Goldbart 1998) will continue to haunt the quality of teaching in SLD schools as we progress through the new millennium. It may have been that, during the 1990s, teachers in SLD schools were indeed guilty of compromising the needs of their pupils as they struggled to implement the National Curriculum. If that was the case, then the corporate guilt of teachers in

SLD schools could be explained and softened by their desire at the time to uphold the rights of entitlement of their pupils at all costs, even when they were aware of the shortcomings of that entitlement. However, the term 'inclusion' has largely replaced 'entitlement' as the buzz-word of special education as we progress into the first decade of the new millennium. The use of P levels has strengthened the idea that the National Curriculum is an inclusive curriculum with the capacity to meet the needs of all pupils. In turn, the notion that the National Curriculum is a curriculum for inclusion has considerably weakened arguments for promoting specialist curricula in response to the needs of disabled pupils. There can be no excuse made for those SLD practitioners who have sought to force the issue of establishing P levels as the principal means of defining the whole curriculum for pupils with SLD/PMLD.

In the quasi-commercial world of education in the 21st century, value-added criteria will increasingly be used as a fundamental means of appraising school effectiveness and for determining the performance-related pay of teachers. The under-developed measures for evaluating special-school performance, reported by OFSTED (Sebba *et al.* 1996), have clearly been a nuisance for developing value-added criteria in the SLD sector. However, P levels would have the potential for providing such data and, by linking teacher performance with P levels, the DfEE could ensure that the implementation of P levels can be given the highest priority in SLD schools, regardless of whether or not P levels represented good SLD practice.

Raising the status of P levels has re-invoked the idea that the National Curriculum is an entitlement curriculum and has the power to secure the social inclusion of disabled children. This enduring belief in the power of the National Curriculum comes about as an emotional response to the sad history of social injustice dealt out to disabled children prior to 1970, but it has little relevance to the quasi commercial world of 21st-century education. However, it is a belief that could result in the use of P levels as the primary source of value-added criteria and the subsequent failure of SLD schools to address properly the holistic needs of their pupils.

It is important that the dogma of inclusion is not allowed to mask the real needs of pupils with SLD/PMLD in the same manner that the dogma of entitlement was allowed to do so during the 1990s. The National Curriculum was not developed with the needs of all school pupils in mind (Powell and Jordan 1998), and as such it should not be regarded as a curriculum that can be used to enable the social inclusion of pupils with profound and complex disabilities, nor as the primary means of appraising practice in the SLD sector. This is regardless of whether or not the National Curriculum has been modified through the addition of P levels.

When one seeks to advocate that pupils with SLD/PMLD deserve to benefit from discreet attention, then, almost inevitably, there will be those who condemn such advocacy and deny the promotion of positive discrimination. Indeed, there have been authors who have described SLD/PMLD advocates as wanting to perpetuate some kind of special-needs industry (Oliver 1996). If ever there is such an industry being perpetuated, surely the situation has not arisen with commercial viability in mind, because the small numbers of pupils involved represent a very limited commercial prospect. The SEN industry, which exists around the education and care for pupils with SLD/PMLD is perpetuated only because there will always be some children who require a specialist sheltered environment (Tilstone 1996). The needs of some disabled children are radically different from those of the average child. These different needs must be given proper status, and SLD practitioners need to be encouraged to make special provision in response to those needs rather than be criticised for failing to observe the dogma issued by government spin-doctors and academics, who carry no public accountability for the viability or quality of the dogma they advance.

All of this is not to say that provision for pupils with SLD/PMLD ought to be segregated provision or that it should not be governed by a national strategy that ensures public accountability for the quality of specialist provision. The dilemma currently facing SLD schools is perhaps greater than that faced by any other SEN sector. The scale of this dilemma has come about as a consequence of the ever-growing complexity, diversity and acute nature of the disabilities that are now typical of pupils with SLD/PMLD (Aird 2000a). Provision for these pupils is not limited to services provided by LEAs and managed by the DfEE but is also intrinsically linked with services provided by local health authorities and social services departments. The holistic needs of pupils with SLD/PMLD must be paramount when developments in specialist provision are considered.

It is likely that, with a growing emphasis upon school league tables that are based upon pupil performance within the narrow constraints of the National Curriculum, pupils with the most profound and complex disabilities may well suffer greater social exclusion than that experienced at any time since 1970. In 1997, The Mental Health Foundation reported that an increasing emphasis on structured teaching situations in special schools, associated with the National Curriculum, could cause problems for pupils with additional so-called 'severe challenging behaviour' and result in an increase in the social exclusion of these pupils. Evidence of increased social exclusion of disabled children, as a consequence of ERA88 and its aftermath, has been provided by the Department of Health and

Social Services Inspectorate (1993), Barnardos (1995) and Morris (1995). SLD schools are becoming too complex and are being required to adopt too many peripheral practices to be able to respond properly to the demands of their pupils. An obvious outcome for many pupils who have severely challenging behaviour or profound disability will be exclusion or transfer to specialist, residential schools.

The leadership and organisation of SLD schools

ERA88 made the management of all schools, including SLD schools, considerably more complex than they were previously (West and Ainscow 1991). The tasks of becoming financially self-managing, implementing the National Curriculum and responding to a plethora of other changes in school management presented head teachers and governors – including those in charge of SLD schools – with challenges that they barely had time to respond to before being required to consider other changes. Since ERA88, the scale of educational reform has not lessened, and for many head teachers it has felt as if these constant changes were introduced with the sole intention of denying them the opportunity to feel in control of their own schools. Frustratingly, in addition to the trend for maintaining schools in a state of constant flux, successive Secretaries of State have also tended to want to make educational changes happen as quickly as possible.

For SLD schools, this situation has meant that requirements have become more complex and have involved an increasingly diverse range of specialist services. At the same time, the head teachers of these schools have become increasingly more accountable for the quality of their school's provision in areas far removed from the traditional role of such specialist and multi-agency establishments. It is hardly surprising that increasing numbers of LEAs report difficulties in recruiting head teachers and governors for SLD schools. These recruitment difficulties are a symptom of an education system that has become increasingly driven by political whim. The leadership of schools has become a primary focus of scrutiny by OFSTED, and no doubt many of the head teachers who became casualties in the first two rounds of special-school OFSTED inspections did so not because of a lack of ability but rather because they were unable to make sense of the scale of educational reforms quite as quickly – or, perhaps, as unquestioningly – as other head teachers. School heads have been required to participate in educational reforms or face the consequences.

ERA88 changed the role of head teachers in SLD schools from that of curriculum leader to that of multi-tasked manager. However, ERA88 neglected to bring online all of the concepts, understandings and skills that head teachers would require in order to fulfil their new role. It should not have been a surprise, therefore, that many head teachers found it difficult to fulfil this new role and maintain the standard of specialist provision they might have wished for. Since 1988, there have been efforts to establish a national job description and a route for senior teachers to be trained toward the role of head teacher, but there has been no discreet attention directed towards the specific needs of head teachers in SLD schools, who have to manage complex multi-agency environments.

The changing role of the head teacher has brought with it a real risk that head teachers may have become too distanced from their staff, pupils and curriculum as a consequence of their preoccupation with managerial activities (Styan *et al.* 1990). Such a situation ought not to be tolerated in the complex SLD school where the head teacher's personal knowledge can be vital for ensuring a child's well-being. The various duties that a head teacher is now required to undertake does not make it easy to judge whether the head teacher of an SLD school is an effective leader or not. For example, a head teacher may be effective in managing a school's budget but may not be as effective in managing a school's curriculum, in maintaining good standards of teaching and learning, and/or in working in partnership with supporting professionals.

The tense and changing world of school management is important when one considers the future of SLD schools. ERA88 has been described as legislation that offered schools the capacity simply to disappear (Fidler 1989). This is because, having empowered schools with the ability to become self-determining in specific aspects of their management, such as financial control, the same legislation also brought with it public accountability. Schools that have been deemed by OFSTED as being ineffective are labelled as having serious weaknesses, or being in need of special measures; they either have to improve their effectiveness or face closure. Given that special schools have been noted for having among them a relatively high percentage with serious weaknesses and in need of special measures (OFSTED 1998), the question of what makes a special school an effective school poses a fundamental challenge for those who manage special schools and, particularly, for the head teachers of SLD schools, who need to make provision for the holistic needs of their pupils. Meeting the holistic needs of pupils is not a high priority under the current framework of school inspection, and there are very few criteria available to OFSTED for knowing how to judge value for money and effectiveness in areas involving profound disability and acute health impairment.

SLD schools have only been in existence for some thirty years and, for the most recent ten or so, attention to what makes an SLD school effective (or not) has tended to be directed via a system of school appraisal that was developed for mainstream schools. This is despite SLD schools being reported as having become increasingly more complex (OFSTED 1998), thereby requiring more complex ways of appraising their effectiveness. The failure to recognise that SLD schools are different from all other types of school has been an unfortunate recurring feature within national strategy. A good example of this kind of failure was much in evidence in the publication entitled *Meeting Special Educational Needs: a Programme of Action* (DfEE 1998). Despite specifically having an SEN focus, this important document had no advice to offer about what criteria can be used to judge whether SLD schools are being as effective as they might be in educating, caring for and treating children with complex disabilities.

Although there has been some occasional ad-hoc guidance, such as *Planning the Curriculum for Pupils with Profound and Multiple Learning Difficulties* (SCAA 1996b) and *Shared World – Different Experiences: Designing the Curriculum for Pupils who are Deafblind* (QCA 1999), documents such as these have had a very narrow focus and have provided little advice in helping identify good practice in SLD schools. Throughout the advice given, there has always been the notion that teaching and learning in SLD schools needs to conform with the national model and operate within the framework that was developed by our society for organising mainstream education – a model that was developed by people with little knowledge or understanding of children with disabilities (Sebba *et al.* 1995). This notion of conformity threatens the very nature of the SLD school. The insistence that SLD schools conform in this crude way risks denying pupils with SLD/PMLD the means by which they should be able to exercise their true capabilities (Sutherland 1981).

This would not be the case if there was a clear national strategy for the development of SLD schools – a strategy that was clearly based upon the needs, rights and aspirations of severely and profoundly disabled children and their families, and one that benefited from multi-agency collaboration. In the next chapters, there is an attempt to provide clarity of purpose for SLD schools. There are practical suggestions as to how the diverse and often unique elements of SLD schools' management can be addressed in a coherent and holistic manner, without the risk of marginalising SLD schools to the extent that they would need to exist outside the state education system.

There is much wrong with the current system that prevents good SLD practice from being nurtured, and this opening chapter has sought to describe some of the aspects that have not gone well for the SLD sector over the past decade or so. At the current time there appears to be a national lack of clarity about what it is that actually defines 'good practice' in the education, care and treatment of pupils with

SLD/PMLD. It is likely that this lack of clarity has much to do with the continued use of the phrase 'learning difficulty' as a means of labelling pupils who have severe or profound disabilities. A learning difficulty suggests varying degrees of difficulty that may delay a child's attainment of normal developmental milestones but that will not greatly inhibit such attainment over time. Hence, the focus of attention in recent times has been on the careful differentiation of the norm-referenced National Curriculum, with the intention of enabling pupils with SLD/PMLD to access the same kinds of skills and knowledge as their non-SEN peers, albeit at a slower rate.

However, in addition to their underlying learning difficulties, pupils with SLD/PMLD also have severe, profound and complex disabilities that require specialist curricula far removed from the National Curriculum and requiring methodologies of teaching and care that are as idiosyncratic as the disabilities themselves. To compromise a child's disability is to handicap that child for life, and SLD schools must never allow themselves to make such a compromise for want of being seen to conform to national mainstream frameworks. A pupil's school life is a brief affair, and the time in the classroom is a precious time that ought to be dedicated to minimising the handicapping affects of a pupil's disability and enabling the pupil to achieve maximum potential in a broad but relevant curriculum that is unique to the SLD sector and does not smack of the tokenism that has marred the history of the implementation of the National Curriculum in the SLD sector thus far (Byers 1999).

CHAPTER 2

Strategies for securing clarity of purpose

Clarity of pupils' personal learning styles

Clarity is something to do with having good vision – something about having the ability to perceive things as they truly are. Clarity of purpose in the SLD sector ought to begin with perceiving the rights, needs and aspirations of children with severe, profound and complex disabilities as they truly are. The need for clarity of purpose in the SEN sector is nothing new and, in 1992, HMI advised that there will never be answers to the problems posed by making provision for SEN until there is an adequate working definition of SEN and a more effective system of accountability (Audit Commission and HMI 1992a, 1992b). In the absence of any subsequent advice about what might constitute a working definition of SEN, it ought not to be presumptuous of SLD schools to begin formulating their own working definition of what it is that constitutes SLD provision.

It is some time since the notion was advanced that individual handicaps are both relative and situational (Fish 1985, 1989). Handicaps have various characteristics and degrees of severity, which are caused not by the presence of disabilities or impairments but by the situation in which disabled children find themselves. Fish declared (1989) that the operational basis for defining SEN must be in the variations that are found in the essential characteristics of different disability types and the degree to which these characteristics might become handicapping, or not, dependent upon the provision that is made available. If we accept Fish's working definition of the operational basis for SEN provision, then we begin to appreciate that the extent of a child's handicap in the classroom is largely determined by how well the school's environment for teaching and learning has been designed to respond empathetically to the characteristics of particular disability types – in other words, how effective a school is in recognising and responding to the individual needs of its pupils.

Within a typical SLD school, there will be pupils on roll with all manner of disability types at all levels of severity. It is not easy, therefore, for the average SLD school to formulate a working definition of SLD provision and thus secure clarity of purpose. A child may be labelled as having ASD, Down's Syndrome, Fragile X Chromosome and/or – increasingly commonly in recent times – Attention Deficit Syndrome. However, none of these labels actually helps us to understand what kind of provision a particular pupil might require in order to minimise the handicapping effect of his or her disabilities and allow good general progress.

With experience, one may be able to refer to a pupil's clinical diagnosis of disability and 'get a feel' for the kind of SEN provision that the pupil might require as a consequence of the innate disability. However, such responses to disability are largely subjective and too generalised to be of real value in a classroom. A common diagnosis of cerebral palsy in two infants, for example, does not mean that both children will have the same characteristics, likes, dislikes, preferences, periods of good health – or even the same special educational needs. Neither does it mean that both children will have the same life experiences, as a consequence of their birth trauma, nor that their needs will remain unchanged over time. Having recognised that pupils who share a common diagnosis are more likely than not to have different needs, it follows that there can be no single teaching approach that can be used to meet those needs (Smith 1991). When one considers the broad spectrum of disability types, typical of pupils on roll at an average SLD school, one can begin to get an impression of the huge task facing these schools as they struggle to organise effective specialist provision.

DFE Circular 22/89 (1989) advised that a child's special school placement ought to be determined after considering whether a nominated school's facilities, equipment, staffing arrangements and curriculum are construed as being appropriate to a child's SEN. It is important, therefore, that a special school has clarity of purpose and is coherent and unambiguous when it comes to defining its SEN provision. Clarity of purpose for the SLD school begins by having an intimate knowledge of the idiosyncratic characteristics of each pupil's disabilities, supported by absolute clarity about what the educational, caring and treatment implications of these characteristics are, in order that the school environment can be organised to work empathetically with the characteristics of pupils on roll (Aird and Lister 1999).

The environmental context to disability is fundamental for enabling effective learning to take place (Goldsmith and Goldsmith 1998). It ought not to be unreasonable, therefore, to expect that an SLD school that specialises in the teaching of pupils with diverse and complex disabilities will recognise the importance of keeping the characteristics of its pupils central to its planning (Sanderson *et al.* 1997). The characteristics of pupils with SLD/PMLD have many implications for the way in which specialist provision should be organised to ensure optimum effectiveness in the classroom. The ways in which specialist provision needs to be organised in SLD schools, therefore, are complex and diverse. What is required is a system for classifying all of these implications and analysing how they make an impact upon various dimensions of school organisation, so that provision can be organised in a logical manner.

The implications of disability may be considered as being multi-dimensional in the ways in which they have an effect upon school organisation (Aird and Bainbridge 1997). The content, design and organisation of the curriculum, for example, need to be heavily influenced by the educational implications of disability if pupils are going to be allowed the opportunity to learn effectively (Brown *et al.* 1998). There are also immediate implications for the types of teaching methodologies that need to be employed in the school, the range of facilities that the school will need to make available, and the types of links with other agencies that will need to be maintained in order to respond to the non-educational implications of disability, such as a child's care and treatment regimes.

There is a well-known visual illusion called the Necker Cube, which is a line drawing that the brain interprets as representing a three-dimensional cube. The interesting thing about the Necker Cube is that there are two possible orientations that the brain can interpret. Although these orientations make the cube look different on separate occasions, both orientations are equally compatible with the two-dimensional line drawing given. The design of the Necker Cube enables a person to interpret the same basic information in two distinct ways, with each interpretation having the same intrinsic value and relationship to the original line drawing.

The Necker Cube illusion has been used to illustrate an approach for managing the education and care of pupils with SLD/PMLD so as to ensure that a school's organisation reflects the needs of its pupils (Aird and Bainbridge 1997). In other words, information about disability can be used in two ways:

- to define what is special about a child's disability in terms of the implications for teaching, learning, caring and treatment;
- to define what is special about a school's organisation in terms of its curriculum, staffing, environment and multi-agency collaboration.

In order to implement the Necker Cube analogy within the organisation of an SLD school, it is first necessary to audit all of the idiosyncratic characteristics that typify the special needs of the pupils on roll (referred to in this text as a pupil's 'personal learning style') and then determine what the implications of these characteristics will be for:

- the design and content of a curriculum in order to maximise the learning potential of pupils and to ensure that what is taught will be relevant to the personal learning styles of the pupils on roll;
- the knowledge, understanding and specialist teaching/caring/therapeutic skills that will be required by staff in order to work empathetically with each pupil's personal learning style;
- the design features of the teaching environment that will work to minimise the handicapping effect of specific disabilities and provide a safe, secure and enabling environment;
- the use of specialist resources and personal aids to empower pupils and help make their learning as autonomous as possible;
- the networking with parents, specialist support agencies and voluntary organisations that will be required to ensure that a pupil's holistic needs are properly accounted for.

There is no off-the-shelf pack that a school can use to advise it about this process of audit, and it will be necessary for the school's staff and supporting professionals to work together in shaping such an audit. Individual staff members will need to pool their knowledge about each pupil in order to identify the pertinent characteristics of each pupil's personal learning style. The value of involving staff directly in tasks relating to school development (such as conducting an audit) has long been established, particularly as a means of motivating staff (Steers and Porter 1983) and helping staff agree what a school's priorities should be (Bush 1986). There are powerful arguments for taking a close look at the various characteristics that typify the personal learning styles of pupils on roll and sharing what the implications are likely to be for the way in which the school needs to be organised.

Knowledge about the personal learning styles of pupils on roll and their associated implications for specialist provision will come from a number of sources and will vary in the type of evidence that staff use to substantiate such knowledge. For instance, some knowledge will be based upon evidence that is empirical. Some knowledge about a pupil with PMLD, for example, may be obtained from a physiotherapist who will have empirical evidence about a pupil's physiological characteristics and ways in which that pupil needs to be engaged in therapeutic exercises and supported to ensure good posture. A speech therapist will have empirical evidence about a pupil's characteristic swallowing difficulties and the implications of these characteristics for the way that the pupil should be given food and drink in order to avoid the aspiration of foodstuffs into the lungs. A paediatrician will have empirical evidence about a pupil's general health and the implications of specific health difficulties for the way in which that pupil needs to be cared for in order to maintain their general well-being.

Some knowledge will not be supported by empirical evidence, however, but will be largely anecdotal. For example, it is likely that Teaching Assistants (TAs) will develop good knowledge about a pupil's preferences and modes of communicating essential messages, such as discomfort. This knowledge is developed by having regular and intimate contact with a pupil and learning to recognise subtle changes in the pupil's behaviour that other adults, with less frequent contact, may be unaware of. These personal characteristics are not directly linked with any particular disability or impairment, and knowledge about them will be anecdotal. However, the implications of recognising such characteristics can be very significant in terms of the specialist provision that ought to be developed in response to a pupil's personal circumstances. Knowing about an individual pupil's idiosyncratic ways of indicating likes and dislikes is a good starting point for shaping a total communication strategy, and it ought to be given high status when a school is considering its specialist provision for pupils with PMLD.

Regardless of whether knowledge about a pupil's personal learning style is based on empirical or anecdotal evidence, all knowledge needs to be granted equal importance in order that a pupil's holistic needs may be given proper consideration. Multi-agency collaboration is a prerequisite for conducting such an audit because the circumstances of pupils with SLD/PMLD dictate that no one person can ever hope to be able to identify, let alone fully comprehend, the extent of an individual pupil's disabilities and what the implications of these disabilities might be for their education and care (Lacey 1998).

The exercises that follow have been developed to serve as prompts for a school's staff to pool their knowledge of the pupils on roll and begin to interpret what the implications of this knowledge might be for the development of specialist provision at school. The prompts have been designed deliberately to cross over the various undefined boundaries that exist between the different agencies that are involved in the education, care and treatment of children with SLD/PMLD, and to stimulate the sharing of specialist knowledge between adults.

Exercise 1: To agree characteristics that are typical of particular disability types

The first exercise focuses upon the sharing of knowledge about pupils who have been identified as having the same clinical diagnosis. This medical approach is deliberate and is intended to ensure that professionals who are expert in specific aspects of disability are able to contribute to school development planning without feeling that their clinical knowledge is not valued in an educational environment. It is also intended to demonstrate that no one particular regime of treatment or education should be used in isolation.

Context

It is important that a school's staff, as well as members of the various agencies who support pupils at the school, work together in order to identify and agree the major disability types that are most prevalent within a school's population. A selection of disability types might include:

- multi-sensory impairment (MSI);
- profound, multiple learning difficulties (PMLD);
- autistic spectrum disorder (ASD);
- severe challenging behaviour.

Remember that the purpose of this exercise is not to classify pupils according to any crude disability types, because that sort of information has little tangible benefit in the classroom. The purpose of the exercise is to provide a real-life focus for collecting information about the actual characteristics of pupils who are either diagnosed as having specific disabilities and/or who have been described as having a particular type of SEN. The labelling of the various disability types is largely irrelevant and can be left to staff teams to agree. It is the actual characteristics that are common to particular disability types that are of real interest, because it is this information that will be used to provide information for subsequent SEN planning on a whole-school basis and also on an individual-pupil basis.

By focusing attention upon what is known about the characteristics of individual pupils, this exercise allows staff to contribute anecdotal knowledge about a pupil's special needs without necessarily having any specialist knowledge about the particular disability under consideration. However, the team involved in carrying out the exercise needs to have some individual team members who have a good specialist knowledge about the aetiology of specific disability types, and it may also need access to specialist source material, in order to help guide the team in its research. The exercise will also require a list of all pupils who have been diagnosed with a specific disability type and/or who are described as having a particular SEN, in order to prompt real-life interpretations about what is already known about these pupils' personal learning styles.

It is more than likely that, during this exercise, some pupils will be labelled with more than one disability type (eg. severe challenging behaviour and ASD). This is quite acceptable and helps to emphasise the complex nature of each pupil's personal learning style

Prerequisite resources and materials

In order to ascertain the prerequisite resources and materials necessary for auditing the schools' pupils with their particular disabilities, you will need:

- a list of particular disability types that are to be audited;
- A list of pupils who are known to have particular types of SEN;
- source materials such as Statements of SEN, assessment reports, and Annual Review reports, in addition to any authoritative texts on particular disabilities that are felt to be useful;
- an audit team, comprising teaching and support staff, staff with specialist knowledge about specific disability types, professionals from supporting agencies who have specialist knowledge, and parents/carers of the pupils being reviewed;
- an audit prompt sheet with which to shape discussions (such as the generic prompt sheet reproduced as Figure 2.1).

Conducting the audit

A team leader needs to be chosen, whose job it is to set out the terms of reference for conducting the audit. These terms of reference need to describe common characteristics of the disability type being audited and how some of these characteristics may be identified in the behaviour and personal learning styles of certain pupils on the roll. Other team members are then required to contribute to the terms of reference by referring to source materials or simply by using their personal knowledge of individual pupils who are known to have the particular diagnosis in question.

The team leader should keep discussions focused by classifying the characteristics of pupils against prompts contained within an audit prompt sheet. The

Prompt sheet for auditing the characteristics of particular disability types

Disability type under consideration:

Describe the characteristics/behaviours of pupils as they are demonstrated in different settings

1. How does the pupil respond to different physical environments and are there any known preferences/dislikes?

2. Does the pupil's physical condition and/or health result in any discomfort and/or pain and are there any known preferences/dislikes regarding how the pupil is managed physically?

3. How does the pupil behave when he/she is comfortably accommodated within a room but left to their own devices?

4. How does the pupil respond to adults/peers and are there any known preferences/dislikes regarding how inter-personal activities are conducted?

5. How refined are the pupil's communication and language skills?

6. Does the pupil ever become anxious and/or show distress at different times of the day, during different activities, in particular rooms, with particular adults/pupils?

7. How does the pupil express preferences or state an opinion?

8. Does the pupil ever display aggressive behaviours towards themselves or others and if so, when and in what settings do these most often occur?

9. Is the pupil aware of basic rules and routines in the classroom?

10. How mobile is the pupil and how would you describe their physical abilities?

11. How refined are the pupil's fine motor skills, for instance how well can he/she grasp small objects, twist, turn, push, pull objects, manipulate a pencil etc.?

12. How does the pupil use their basic senses of vision, hearing, touch, taste and smell and are there any known preferences/dislikes?

13. How does the pupil best learn new skills, is it by listening to verbal commands, observing modelled behaviour, inter-active prompts or by some other means?

14. How autonomous is the pupil in his/her daily living skills?

15. How logical would you say the pupil is and does he/she have any demonstrable numeracy skills?

16. At what levels within the various subjects of the National Curriculum would you say the pupil is working at?

17. Does the pupil have any personal aspirations and is he/she able to advocate these effectively?

Figure 2.1 Generic prompt sheet for auditing the characteristics of particular disability types

content of a prompt sheet will be largely dependent upon the degree of clarity required by a particular school. For instance, for the specific purpose of auditing characteristics of pupils with ASD at Baginton Fields School in Coventry, a very detailed audit sheet of some 59 behaviours, relating to the triad of impairment (Wing 1998), was used in order to ascertain an accurate overview of the range of the prevalent characteristics of pupils attending the school who had been diagnosed as having ASD.

It is best that schools devise their own audit sheets, following research and consultation with relevant specialists, rather than rely upon a set of generic prompts. However, where time and resource are of the essence, the use of a generic audit sheet, such as the example provided in Figure 2.1, has the potential to yield much information that can be put to good use, particularly for ascertaining the personal learning styles of individual pupils. It is important that an audit prompt sheet is as holistic as possible in its scope and incorporates prompts that may help to describe a pupil's characteristics within:

- pre-verbal stages of development;
- basic communication skills;
- emotional and behavioural development;
- physical and motor abilities;
- sensory and perceptual abilities;
- independent living skills;
- health and well-being;
- self-advocacy;
- basic cognitive and academic abilities.

By the end of this initial audit exercise, a considerable amount of information will have been amassed about individual pupils and about the prevalent characteristics of particular disability types. Returning to the analogy of the Necker Cube, this same information can be used for two separate, but closely linked, purposes:

1. to help engender embryonic profiles of personal learning styles on behalf of individual pupils (as described below);
2. to be taken forward for further classification and analysis on a whole-school basis (as described in Chapter 3).

Exercise 2: To analyse a pupil's individual characteristics

Context

Having established a good bank of information about the various characteristics and behaviours of pupils on roll, this information may then be subjected to further classification and subsequently analysed, so that the implications of these characteristics can be considered within various contextual dimensions that are representative of the way in which SLD schools are organised. The Necker Cube analogy gives rise to four such contextual dimensions:

- the design and content of the whole curriculum;
- the skills and knowledge of the staff, and the methodologies they use;
- the design of resources, facilities and the school's physical environment;
- the skills and knowledge of specialist supporting agencies, and how the school collaborates with these specialists.

Prerequisite resources and materials

The prerequisites for this exercise are:

- sets of raw information about the characteristics of individual pupils as they relate to specific disabilities, loosely classified under the headings provided by audit prompt sheets;
- blank sheets with which to transfer and collate information about individual pupil's characteristics, as identified during the audit of specific disabilities;
- blank copies of the Dimensions of Disability Audit Sheet (see Figure 2.2 for a partially completed example) with which to analyse the implications of each pupil's characteristics according to the dimensions of disability.

Conducting the analysis

The lists of characteristics and behaviours generated on behalf of each individual pupil should be collated. The team leader might wish to bring together all of the information about an individual pupil, as identified during separate audits of disability, and combine these separate audit findings on a fresh sheet so as to present a more holistic overview of an individual pupil's characteristics.

The team leader will need to model how the implications of particular characteristics can be interpreted by reference to the four dimensions of disability

Dimensions of Disability Audit Sheet

Dimensions ➡ Characteristics ⬇	Whole curriculum	Staffing	Resource/ facility	Support services
Pupil becomes aggressive and violent when routines change	1. Specialist curricula to develop pupil's ability to cope with anxiety and anger (emotional, behavioural and social education) 2. Cross-curricular total communication strategy	1. Staff need skills to manage challenging behaviour and physical intervention 2. Staff need to be consistent	1. PECs and/or cues to support pupil before changes in routine occur 2. Discreet curriculum time for emotional and behavioural development	1. Support from clinical psychologist about use of physical interventions 2. Advice from speech therapist about use of PECS
Pupil cannot eat unaided and chokes if food is not liquidised to the preferred consistency	1. Opportunities for the pupil to express preferences between different tastes and textures 2. Opportunities to express preferences about how food is offered	1. Staff need to have good knowledge of eating disorders 2. 1:1 Staffing required for giving meals and drinks 3. Staff need to recognise the pupil's way of indicating preferences	1. Detailed instructions about pupil's feeding regime 2. Liquidiser to prepare food as required 3. Angled spoon	1. Assessment of swallow from specialist speech & language therapist 2. Written advice about feeding regime 3. Regular monitoring for aspiration of foodstuffs 4. Advice on communication strategy

Figure 2.2 Example of a partly completed Dimensions of Disability Audit Sheet

listed above. For instance, if a pupil is known to have a characteristic physical impairment, the team leader will need to demonstrate what the implications of this physical impairment might be for:

- the content of the whole curriculum;
- the way in which staff are organised;
- any specific skills the staff might require;
- any special resources staff might need to use;
- collaborations with specialist support agencies.

Once team members are confident about the process of analysing the data they have collated on each pupil, members of the team will need to work their way through the long list of characteristics and interpret the implications of these characteristics within the four contextual dimensions of disability, whilst the team leader records the findings on each pupil's Dimensions of Disability Audit Sheet.

Establishing each pupil's personal learning style

During the course of this exercise, a considerable amount of information will be generated about the characteristics of each pupil and recorded on their individual Dimensions of Disability Audit Sheet. The data from this audit sheet can be used to establish a pupil's personal learning style in a manner that ensures that the relevance of the school's special provisions for an individual pupil will be consistent across all aspects of school organisation. Although it may not be unreasonable to expect class teachers and their supporting TAs to have a good working knowledge and understanding of the individual needs of their pupils, there is still an important need to ensure that information about the personal learning styles of individual pupils is readily accessible in a classroom and is used to assist with lesson planning and everyday pastoral arrangements.

Classrooms in SLD schools are notorious for the number of adults who pass through their doors each day. In addition to the class teacher and supporting TAs, there may be visiting therapists, students, volunteers, social workers, parents, doctors, nurses, lunchtime supervisory staff and home–school escorts, to name but some. Although contact with individual pupils by these adults may only be for a short period, there is the potential for inappropriate interactions to occur. It is not unusual for pupils who have severe challenging behaviour to react in a confrontational way if they are approached in an unfamiliar manner; nor is it unusual to see a pupil with PMLD startle and go into extension because a visitor has sought to attract his or her attention in an inappropriate way. All adults who have contact with pupils in an SLD school have the potential to assist *or hinder* the education and care of the pupils they are in contact with (Jones 2000). It is imperative that sufficient information is at hand to ensure that such contact is always of the type that will assist in the education and care of pupils.

The value of having information displayed in the manner described above has been well documented, and the concept of 'personal passports' for children with MSI (Hawke and Stanislawski 1999) and ASD (Jones 2000) are good examples of how crucial information can be shared in the classroom. For pupils who are likely to have complex disabilities and who receive services from a large number of professionals, the importance of information sharing is even more vital. For example, a physiotherapist may be knowledgeable about a pupil's characteristics within the area of mobility but would be unlikely to know how to communicate effectively with that same pupil unless pertinent information was readily to hand. How could a physiotherapist know, for instance, whether a pupil was feeling uncomfortable or in pain if the therapist was not aware that a specific yet subtle change in the pupil's behaviour was indicative of such an important message. If there is to be effective multi-agency collaboration in the classroom so as to assist in the holistic education, care and treatment of pupils with SLD/PMLD, then each individual adult coming into contact with these pupils must to some extent be able to function in a multidisciplinary way in order to maintain continuity of provision.

Having clear and unambiguous information about the personal learning styles of pupils can also assist in monitoring the environment, to ensure that setting conditions within a classroom are appropriate for learning to take place (Bull and Solity 1987). A pupil needs to be comfortable, safe and secure in order to be receptive to learning (Goldsmith and Goldsmith 1998), and it is important that there is continuity of environment to enable pupils with PMLD in particular to make sense of the world around them and begin to develop concepts about their place in it (Brown *et al.* 1998). In the absence of any objective empirical evidence that a pupil has learned a new skill or concept, evidence of progress can sometimes only be found in subtle changes in a pupil's behaviour. It is not unusual for staff who work with pupils with PMLD to comment that their pupils do not appear to be benefiting from the activities they are engaged in (Ware 1996). However, where there is good awareness about the subtle idiosyncrasies of a pupil's personal learning style, staff are able to interpret whether a pupil is actively engaged in an activity or has retreated from the activity because the learning environment or teaching methodology is antipathetic to the circumstances.

Teachers in SLD schools have to ensure that their pupils benefit from contact with adults who have the appropriate level of multi-agency expertise to work with them empathetically. Teachers also need to be confident that the classroom environment they manage will work in favour of their pupils, not inhibit them or compound an aspect of their disability. Without the benefit of well-informed, up-to-date and easily accessible personal-learning-style documentation, teachers are not able to facilitate a good quality, or continuity of provision. Interpreting the implications of a pupil's disabilities by reference to dimensional contexts enables practical and accurate documentation to be collated. Whether this documentation is referred to as a pupil's personal learning style, personal passport or care plan is not really important – although the fact that we are considering the organisation of schools, as opposed to other sorts of establishments, suggests that a reference to learning is perhaps more pertinent than references to travel or caring.

The development of personal learning styles represents the way in which we can define SEN on an individual-pupil basis within the SLD school. This is one of the two interpretations afforded by the Necker Cube analogy. The second interpretation relates to how we can define SEN on a whole-school basis. Both interpretations use the same basic information, but one interpretation defines pupil need on an individual basis while the other defines SEN provision on a whole-school basis. In the next chapter, I will discuss the need for SLD schools to secure clarity of purpose on a whole-school basis, as considered against the context of a state education system that is increasingly being influenced by an enterprise culture imported from the world of commerce.

CHAPTER 3

Clarity of purpose for the whole school

The influence of the enterprise culture

In the enterprise culture that is now so much a feature of the modern-day education system, the vocabulary of the business world has been allowed to become increasingly applied to describe the work of schools (Thompson and Barton 1992). Value for money, performance targets, development plans, appraisals and value added are all concepts that have become commonplace in every type of school since ERA88. Simply by listening to media reports about standards in schools, a casual listener may be left with the impression that the fundamental role of schools is synonymous with that of commercial businesses. Despite whatever reassurances we can glean from more familiar terms such as 'entitlement', 'differentiated learning' and an 'inclusive' education system, the increasing influence of the enterprise culture and its innate vocabulary does not and cannot work in favour of pupils with SLD/PMLD.

Vocabulary imported from the world of business, such as the term 'value added', is increasingly being used to describe ways in which the performance of schools can be appraised and compared. The marketplace approach, typified by the publication of school performance tables, is reminiscent of company performance tables used for the exchange of stocks and shares. There appears to be a commonly held belief that the quality of education provided by an individual school can be judged solely upon appraisal of its performance data when compared against the performance of other schools. The school infrastructure required to enable this influence of the enterprise culture to continue to grow in importance relies on the notion that schools can be considered as mini-businesses in which pupil performance is viewed as the end product.

With the government's widely publicised determination to move towards an inclusive education system, it would be appropriate to believe that inclusion would result in considerable improvements in the quality of provision for pupils with SLD/PMLD. However, the influence of the enterprise culture may well work against such a belief coming to fruition, and there is a risk that pupils with disabilities may be rendered invisible in the hierarchy of the inclusive school (Soder 1992). Because of their inability to achieve academic standards in accordance with their chronological age, pupils with SLD/PMLD are unlikely to be granted any real status in a school ethos that is geared towards producing academic excellence. As SLD practitioners are all too well aware, academic excellence is not a characteristic of pupils who have severe, profound and complex disabilities, and it is unlikely that any kind of status will be afforded these pupils.

Mainstream schools are increasingly under pressure to raise the academic standards of their pupils, and in such a culture it is inevitable that there will be an ideological gap opened between the status afforded to pupils who are able to attain academic excellence and those who are not (Valachou 1997). It is quite likely that pupils with SLD/PMLD would be marginalised in such a culture, resulting in a more profound sense of segregation for these pupils than would be the case if they attended their local SLD school where they would enjoy a much higher status. The most worrying scenario associated with including pupils with SLD/PMLD within the enterprise culture is that the most profoundly disabled pupils of the United Kingdom would once again become segregated from the state education system. Academic excellence is typified by the ability of pupils to demonstrate autonomy in their mastery of skills, knowledge and concepts that are taught by reference to the framework of the National Curriculum. The profound disabilities of pupils with PMLD make autonomous learning impossible, and these pupils need to rely upon the intervention of others to either carry out basic tasks coactively or have adults serve as their advocates and carry out tasks on their behalf. This inability to demonstrate autonomy in learning would render pupils with PMLD of little or no benefit to schools who are competing in the marketplace of academic excellence. This is a sobering thought for those who would like to see P levels used for the purpose of generating value-added data with which to judge the performance of schools that cater for pupils with SLD/PMLD.

Ensuring that the performance of pupils with SLD/PMLD is recognised and properly valued is not going to be easily secured in a society that only tends to acknowledge achievement in a competitive way, by means of comparing one pupil's achievement with that of others. Society as a whole rarely judges the status of a person's achievements in isolation, and there are serious shortcomings in the means by which society currently appraises the performance of pupils with SLD/PMLD and the effectiveness of their host schools. The means that exist currently for appraising the performance of individual pupils, and the effectiveness of schools in general, are intrinsically linked to the enterprise culture. For instance, the National Curriculum was largely designed in order to provide pupils with the skills and knowledge necessary for employment and for the ultimate goal of generating wealth for the benefit of society in general. Society invests in the education of pupils with the expectation that this investment will realise a sound financial return as pupils attain academic excellence and go on to secure employment.

Given the extent to which the enterprise culture has influenced and infiltrated the education system, segregation of the more profoundly disabled pupils becomes an increasing threat. The results from engaging these pupils in the National Curriculum will have minimal value in the marketplace, and pupils with SLD/PMLD are generally unlikely ever to be able to repay the investment that society has made in their education. The combination of poor academic attainment and continuing reliance upon others for the servicing of their basic needs, inhibits and, on occasion, prohibits many disabled adults from participating in the world of commerce. Clearly, something needs to be done to enable the circumstances of pupils with severe disabilities to be properly valued within the enterprise culture that now pervades the state education system.

Ensuring that pupils with SLD/PMLD are not socially excluded and that SLD schools will be able to continue to function within the current state education system are both things that need to be done without compromising the needs of pupils with SLD/PMLD. Seeking to simplify the National Curriculum to an extent where it may be better suited to the abilities of some pupils with SLD/PMLD is not the answer, despite the fact that it is pupil performance within the National Curriculum that is used to judge school effectiveness. There is a point where oversimplification of the content of subjects of the National Curriculum renders any proposed, differentiated, content unrecognisable as belonging to any particular subject and, as such, the attainment of pupils within this modified curriculum would have little public status. Attempts to use P level curricula in a developmental way, in order to demonstrate levels of achievement in the National Curriculum, has no proven scientific basis and is unlikely to be of any real value for appraising the performance of pupils with SLD/PMLD – or the effectiveness of schools funded to educate these pupils.

There needs to be a far more meaningful framework for judging the effectiveness of SLD schools than that which exists currently. The exercises in this chapter are intended to establish the principles by which the effectiveness of educating pupils with SLD/PMLD can be demonstrated in ways that are meaningful and relevant. In Chapter 2 we established first that, in order to fully appreciate the nature of an individual pupil's SEN, it is necessary to identify those particular characteristics and behaviours that are considered to be 'out of the ordinary'. Secondly, the implications of those characteristics need to be analysed so that they can be communicated and addressed appropriately. The performance of an SLD school can only be seriously appraised by its ability to identify, communicate and address the special needs of its pupils.

The audit of disability described in Chapter 2, if completed in full, would provide a school with an extensive set of SEN-related criteria, representative of the special needs of its pupils and which a school might then choose to use to inform its provision for individual pupils. By a process of further classification and analysis, it is possible to use information gained from the audit of disability to initiate a process of school development planning that retains the needs of pupils at its core and that ultimately could provide a coherent overview of a school's strengths, weaknesses and aspirations.

Exercise 3: To agree the further classification of SEN criteria

This third exercise is intended to initiate a process of school development planning that is based primarily upon the special needs of pupils on roll. In the two previous exercises, characteristics typifying the special needs of the pupils on roll were identified and classified by reference to the four dimensions of disability. In this third exercise, those same characteristics (which may now be termed as the school's SEN criteria) are subjected to a process of further classification.

Context

This additional classification exercise again refers to the four dimensions of disability but introduces additional cross-referencing to classifications that are described as elements of disability. The labels that are selected by a school to represent the elements of disability are a matter of choice, but experience has shown that reference to the following elements is helpful for clarifying the implications of special needs as they relate to crucial aspects of school organisation:

- academic cross-curricular skills (literacy, numeracy, information and communications technology) and P levels from subjects within the National Curriculum;
- specialist curricula relating to specific disability types, which are in addition to the National Curriculum (particularly the educational implications of motor difficulty, sensory impairment, and emotional and behavioural difficulty);

- caring, therapeutic and treatment regimes;
- cross-curricular elements, such as total communication strategies;
- domestic, home–school transport and vocational elements.

Prerequisite resources and materials

The following are the prerequisites for this exercise:

- lists of SEN criteria from Exercises 1 and 2, relating to specific disabilities that have been classified according to the four dimensions of disability;
- copies of blank matrix sheets (see Figure 3.1) with which to undertake further classification of the SEN criteria.

Conducting the reclassification

Once a choice of labels has been agreed upon to represent the elements of disability, a matrix of SEN criteria can then be constructed from which both school aims and developmental priorities can ultimately be drawn. The matrix is constructed along two interrelated axes. Down the left-hand side of the matrix, running in rows across the matrix, are displayed the five elements listed above as crucial to school organisation in relation to special needs. Along the top of the matrix and running vertically down it in columns are displayed the contextual dimensions of disability. A template with which to display information about the whole-school management of disability is shown in Figure 3.1.

SEN criteria, brought forward from Exercise 2, need to be considered as a whole. Preliminary work can be undertaken to organise this material according to how it might correspond to the elements of disability. Any criteria that is duplicated can be discarded, in order to leave a long list of SEN criteria that summarises all the special needs that exist within the school's population.

The team undertaking this third exercise needs to consider each criterion from the list of SEN criteria and place it on the matrix according to which element is considered by the team to be most closely associated. It is likely that some criteria will be relevant to more than one element, and discussions between team members should be encouraged to facilitate this concept. The processes included in this exercise are designed to stimulate discussion between team members and thus promote multi-agency collaboration.

Completion of Exercise 3 will provide a school with SEN criteria that has been classified according to how the information might relate to the five elements of school organisation, together with an illustration of what the implications of this

Whole-School Management of Disability Matrix				
Dimensions ➡ Elements ⬇	Whole curriculum	Staffing	Resource/ facility	Support services
Cross-curricular academic skills and P level curricula				
Specialist curricula				
Caring, therapeutic & treatment regimes				
Cross curricular skills e.g. total commun-ication strategies				
Domestic, home–school transport and vocational elements				

Figure 3.1 Whole-School Management of Disability Matrix

information might be for: the design and content of the whole curriculum; the organisation of staffing; the design and organisation of resources, facilities and the school's physical environment; and any necessary collaboration with specialist support services.

Some rewording of individual SEN criteria may be necessary in order to provide text of a succinct nature that will take up necessarily limited space within the emerging matrix. In Figure 3.2, the SEN criteria from Figure 2.2, an example for Exercise 2, have been brought forward and classified according to the elements of disability. This is to illustrate how the matrix form shown in Figure 3.1 is likely to be completed.

Although simple to execute, Exercise 3 is time-consuming and the final product will undoubtedly be a lengthy document – in the 1997 trial of this exercise, at Baginton Fields School, the resulting document was often referred to as the school's 'SEN wallpaper' because of its length. However, the potential benefits to the school can be very significant, and time given over to completion of the exercise undoubtedly proves to be a good investment: completion of this third exercise provides a school's senior management team (SMT) with networks of interrelated SEN criteria as they are manifested in crucial aspects of school organisation.

Two further exercises are required before the Necker Cube analogy is complete. Exercise 4 relates to the formulation of school aims following summarisation of the SEN criteria developed in Exercise 3. The final exercise includes a process of audit from which the detail of a School Development Plan (SDP) can be constructed.

Exercise 4: To use the matrix of SEN criteria to agree school aims

This exercise is probably best undertaken by a school's SMT rather than with the whole staff. Consultation upon the outcomes of the exercise may then be undertaken with the whole staff team.

Context

A relatively simple task for a school's SMT during Exercise 4 is to rationalise sets of SEN criteria that were classified according to their relationship to the dimensions and elements of disability during Exercise 3. The purpose of this rationalisation is to summarise the information into succinct statements, which can then be used as school aims that have clear links with the education and care of the pupils on roll. The identification of clear aims and values is considered to be fundamental for ensuring an effective school (West and Ainscow 1991) and should be one of the three essential components of an SDP (DES 1989, Gilbert 1992). The remaining two components – considered to be essential for inclusion in an SDP – are references to a school's development needs (which Exercise 5 will help supply), together with any outstanding LEA and national priorities that a school's SMT may feel are appropriate.

Prerequisite resources and materials

The prerequisite resources and materials for this exercise are as follows:

- a completed matrix from Exercise 3, showing SEN criteria classified according to the dimensions and elements of disability;
- a blank sheet of paper with which to record summaries of the SEN criteria allocated to each element, which will then be taken forward as school aims within the SDP.

Conducting the exercise

The exercise comprises three basic steps:

1. The SMT should consider the SEN criteria allocated to each of the various elements and consider whether all the criteria included within a particular element represent a composite set of closely related items or whether some further subdivision may be necessary.
2. Having brought together sets of closely related SEN criteria, the SMT should then agree on succinct statements that summarise the criteria included within each particular set.
3. These summaries may then be considered as the school's aims or mission statements, which will be taken forward for inclusion in Exercise 5 and most likely published in the school prospectus, SDP etc.

Exercise 5: Using the matrix to audit policy and practice

Identifying clear aims for a school's improvement is an important prerequisite for school development planning because of the way in which these aims can aid action planning and the subsequent monitoring of progress (Gilbert 1992). Although the aims of education are similar for all pupils, the aims for an SLD school can be expected to vary from those of other types of school because of the complex characteristics of the pupils on roll. It is important that a school's aims reflect the school's unique philosophy (Fagg *et al.* 1990), and Exercise 4 was developed to ensure that the aims of an SLD school are engendered directly from the special needs of pupils on the roll.

The four exercises presented thus far have been developed to illustrate how the implications of severe and profound disabilities can be interpreted across the various dimensions and elements of school organisation, both on an individual-pupil basis and on a whole-school basis. Clarity about the special needs of the pupils on roll, and about what the implications of these might be for the way in which a school is organised, enables a school's SMT to develop specialist provision in a logical manner and to direct the work of the school according to aims that are meaningful to the whole school community.

This final exercise requires an audit of existing school policy and practice, as considered against the newly defined school aims within the dimensions and elements of school organisation.

Context

Although inclusive school development is generally considered to be an issue for mainstream schools (Booth *et al.* 2000), there is sufficient evidence to suggest that inclusive practice is also an issue within the organisation of SLD schools themselves. One has only to consider the way in which some SLD schools choose to segregate pupils with PMLD, severe challenging behaviour, ASD, etc. to appreciate that inequality of opportunity may be an issue for the pupils who are marginalised in this way.

As this final exercise considers the needs of pupils in relation to whole-school management, issues of inclusion and equality of opportunity are automatically brought to the forefront of a school's SDP. The SDP for a school that caters for pupils with SLD/PMLD needs to be a dynamic document, illustrating the manner in which the school is seeking both to fulfil its aims and to ensure that the needs of all pupils are being addressed appropriately within the management of the whole school.

Completion of this exercise clarifies the extent to which a school is currently meeting the demands of all of its pupils and ensures that there is consistency of provision organised across the whole school, helping to guarantee equality of opportunity.

Prerequisite resources and materials

The following apply as prerequisite resources and materials for Exercise 5:

- a completed matrix of the dimensions and elements of disability;
- a complete set of school aims;
- a whole-school policy and practice audit sheet (see Figure 3.3);
- blank sheets on which to record deficit policies and practice for inclusion in the SDP.

Conducting the audit

There are three main steps to conducting the audit of policy and practice within a school:

1. The newly defined school aims from Exercise 4 need to be recorded within each of the elements on the whole-school policy and practice audit sheet, together with the transfer of all corresponding SEN criteria from the original matrix (see Figures 2.2 and 3.2). Although the transfer of information in this way may prove to be tedious, it serves as a useful opportunity to refine the wording of each criterion and ensure that the sets of criteria are cross-referenced appropriately across the matrix's dimensions

2. When the policy and practice audit matrix is complete, the process of auditing policy may then be undertaken. Each element is taken in turn. The school's SMT needs to consider whether existing school policy is addressing the issues raised by each particular SEN criterion and to record, in the policy column, the titles of existing policies that are felt to be relevant to it. Where policy is felt to be inadequate or absent, these deficits are recorded on a blank sheet of paper and taken forward for inclusion in the SDP.

3. When the audit of school policy is complete, the same procedure may be undertaken with existing practice. Each element is taken in turn and, against each SEN criterion, the SMT must identify whether or not there are examples of good practice in evidence within the organisation of the school. Such examples are recorded on the audit sheet and, where there is no example applicable for an element, this fact is recorded on a separate sheet and taken forward for inclusion in the SDP. It may also become apparent that existing examples of good practice need to be disseminated more widely, and in such cases these items are also taken forward for inclusion in the SDP.

Whole-School Management of Disability Matrix

Dimensions ➡ Elements ⬇	Whole curriculum	Staffing	Resource/ facility	Support services
Cross-curricular academic skills and P level curricula				
Specialist curricula				
Caring, therapeutic & treatment regimes				
Cross-curricular skills e.g. total communication strategies				
Domestic, home–school transport and vocational elements				

SEN criterion (Pupil characteristic brought forward from Exercise 2):
'Pupil becomes aggressive and violent when routines change'

Specialist curricula to develop pupil's ability to cope with anxiety and anger (emotional, behavioural and social education)	3. Staff need skills to manage challenging behaviour 4. Staff need to be consistent	3. PECs and/or cues to support pupil before changes in routine occur 4. Discreet curriculum time for emotional and behavioural development	3. Support from clinical psychologist about use of physical interventions 4. Advice from speech therapist about use of PECS

Figure 3.2 Example of a partly completed Whole-School Management of Disability Matrix

Dimensions ➡ School Aims summarising the SEN criteria included within each element ➡	WHOLE CURRICULUM	Policy	Practice	STAFFING	Policy	Practice	RESOURCE & FACILITIES	Policy	Practice	SPECIAL SUPPORT SERVICES	Policy	Practice
	Cross-curricular academic skills and P level curricula											
	Specialist Curricula											
	Caring, therapeutic and treatment regimes											
	Cross-curricular skills e.g. total communication strategies											
	Domestic, home–school transport and vocational elements											

Figure 3.3 Policy and Practice Audit Sheet

Completion of Exercise 5 provides a school with a good overview of its strengths and weaknesses, as considered against the special needs of its pupils. Policies and areas of practice that are found to be in deficit, or in need of further development, should be taken forward for inclusion within the SDP, thus ensuring that whole-school decision making is based upon the needs of the pupils on roll (Aird and Bainbridge 1997).

Organisation of a school's development plan

In order to provide continuity and coherence within this model of whole-school management, it is helpful if the SDP is also organised by reference to the dimensions and elements of disability. Ideally, the SDP needs to be separated into four sections that relate to the development of:

- design and content of the whole curriculum;
- the organisation of staffing;
- the design and organisation of resources, facilities and the school's physical environment;
- Any necessary collaboration with specialist support services.

Each section of the SDP may then be further subdivided, so as to represent the elements that were agreed during Exercise 2. Overarching this, long-term aims (as shaped during Exercise 4) may be assigned to each of the elements and published in important school documents, such as the school prospectus, to disseminate the school's clarity of purpose to a wider audience. Short-term targets may be readily drawn from the SEN criteria previously classified during Exercise 3, and these targets should in turn be task-analysed so as to tease out the more specific nature of any key tasks that are inherent within each target.

Having completed this work, members of staff may then be nominated to take personal responsibility for specific key tasks, with performance criteria and time lines being agreed with the task leader and budgets allocated to progress the work. Organisation of the SDP in this way enables a school to illustrate how the allocation of cost centres within the school's budget is based upon actual school priorities and how this investment is intended to raise standards (West and Ainscow 1991).

Monitoring the progress of key tasks within the SDP may then be undertaken against a framework of agreed performance indicators and reports fed back to a school's board of governors. The information that a school might use to help clarify the production of personal learning styles on behalf of individual pupils may also be seen to be assisting the production of a SDP and providing clarity of purpose for the whole school community.

Because members of the whole school community are able to be directly involved at all stages throughout this model, ownership of the school's aims and the way in which provision is organised across a school may be readily gained across all sections. Accountability for the school's effectiveness can be clearly demonstrated, on a corporate and an individual staff basis, and multi-agency involvement helps to ensure that the holistic needs of pupils will be properly considered when special provision is being developed. During times when SLD schools are subject to external pressures that have little to do with the actual education and care of disabled children, the Necker Cube approach to school development planning can prove to be a refreshing, highly motivating and rewarding experience.

CHAPTER 4

Keeping pupils at the core of the curriculum

A good starting point

In the late spring of 2000, a document commissioned by the QCA and entitled *Curriculum Guidelines for Pupils Attaining Significantly Below Age-Related Expectation* (Tilstone *et al.* 2000) was circulated to a number of special schools as part of a consultation exercise. The content of that document did not seek to challenge whether the National Curriculum was an appropriate curriculum for pupils with SLD/PMLD, but concentrated instead upon improving the access of pupils with SLD/PMLD to that curriculum by the use of P levels. The consultation document described advantages to be gained from pupils with SLD/PMLD following the same curriculum framework as their non-disabled peers and also suggested that the National Curriculum provided a good starting point for planning the whole curriculum in SLD schools.

The notion that the National Curriculum is able to provide a good starting point for the whole curriculum in an SLD school was a novel idea. Traditionally, it had generally been felt that the curriculum for pupils with SLD/PMLD needed to be fundamentally different from that which was taught to pupils without special needs. Although participation in the National Curriculum had been claimed as being useful for helping prevent SLD schools from being marginalised within the state education system, this benefit had also been stated as being insufficient for engaging pupils with SLD/PMLD in a curriculum that manifestly failed to meet their needs (Ware 1990).

The cautionary note made by Ware in 1990 was in keeping with the views of a long succession of authors, beginning with such noted academics as Tansley and Gulliford (1960), Brennan (1974) and, more recently, by Ouvry (1991) and Sebba *et al.* (1995). The shared view advocated by these authors was that the core and peripheral curricula in mainstream schools needed to be significantly modified in order to be relevant to the needs and abilities of pupils with SEN. The more significant a child's SEN, the greater degree of modification was felt necessary. In particular, this was felt to be the case for pupils with PMLD (Ouvry 1991). The basic framework of the National Curriculum has not changed significantly since its inception and we need to remember that the National Curriculum was designed for mainstream pupils, not for pupils with SLD/PMLD. Following revisions to the National Curriculum in 1994, schools were encouraged to create and maintain their own curriculum, relevant to the needs of the pupils on roll (Marvin 1998). There is little substantive evidence to support the view that the National Curriculum provides a good starting point for the development of the whole curriculum in special schools.

The current obsession with extending the assessment framework of the National Curriculum to include P level curricula is unlikely, in the long run, to be particularly helpful for SLD schools. The reliance upon generalised developmental stages may be appropriate for pupils who are learning-delayed, but such reliance has little relevance for pupils with profound disabilities, whose disabilities largely prohibit their ability to develop along any generalised patterns of development (Brown *et al.* 1998). Linking the assessment of pupils experiencing SLD/PMLD to the framework of the National Curriculum only serves to inhibit the development of an appropriate curriculum for these pupils. It would be far better to recognise the shortcomings of conventional assessment procedures and use a different model of assessment that took into account the idiosyncratic ways in which profoundly disabled children make progress (Barber and Goldbart 1998).

The potential of the National Curriculum to inhibit the delivery of an effective curriculum in special schools received attention during the 1990s when a number of authors – Byers and Rose (1994) and Carpenter and Ashdown (1996) among others – cautioned on the need for special schools to exert more control over their curriculum in the face of external pressures. Their advice built upon concerns first voiced at the beginning of the 1990s, when it was reported that an entitlement to the National Curriculum had the potential to become a rigid restraint for pupils with SLD/PMLD (Norwich 1996). Seeking to establish the National Curriculum and its assessment framework as a good starting point for the development of the SLD school curriculum would only serve to foster that sad façade of academic competence so eloquently described by Barber and Goldbart (1998) and emphasise the inadequacies of profoundly disabled pupils when compared with their non-disabled peers.

Pupils with SLD/PMLD, of course, have a right to access the National Curriculum, but they have more urgent and important rights. A far more meaningful starting point for an SLD school would be the personal learning styles of its

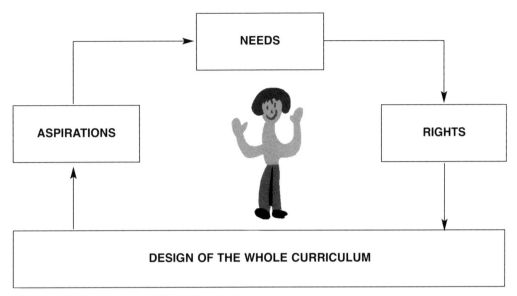

Figure 4.1 A logical order of priorities for the design of the whole curriculum

pupils, and from there the design of a whole curriculum responsive to the aspirations, needs and rights of the pupils on roll (see Figure 4.1).

A good deal has already been written in the opening chapters of this book about the learning characteristics of pupils with SLD/PMLD and how important it is that the education and care of these pupils pays proper attention to these characteristics. Conducting an audit of disability provides a school with good knowledge of the personal learning styles of its pupils and accurate knowledge about the implications of their disabilities for the organisation of the teaching and learning. For example, the personal learning styles of pupils with PMLD are likely to show that these pupils tend to be passive, withdrawn from the world, easily startled and frequently distressed. These characteristics are associated with the implications of MSI, chronic health difficulty, and multiple physical disability – which, for many pupils, combine to severely restrict their ability to interact with the world around them. From the perspective of formulating a curriculum relevant to the needs of these pupils, awareness of their personal learning styles would need to be at the core of a school's curriculum.

Sensory function is reported to play a crucial role in helping babies develop a basic understanding of the properties of the physical world (Warren 1994, Rosen 1997). In order for effective learning to take place, a basic understanding of the properties of the physical world is an absolute prerequisite. Thus, there is a clear link between a child's ability to develop effective sensory function and the ability to learn. When considered in this developmental way, sensory function may rightly be considered as an early step in a pattern of generalised child development that can ultimately lead to the development of skills and knowledge relevant to subjects of the National Curriculum.

However, for many pupils with PMLD, it is unlikely that they will ever be able to develop effective sensory function, and their understanding of the properties of the physical world will remain at a very immature level. The high incidence of sensory impairment in pupils with PMLD means that these pupils are unable to develop any meaningful understanding of the world around them without a tightly controlled and consistent learning environment (Brown *et al.* 1998). The whole curriculum for these pupils does not just start with the need for constant assurance that the world around them is safe, consistent and predictable but also with assurance that it is likely to continue to revolve around these same components for the whole of their school life. As a consequence of their profoundly disabling impairments, pupils with PMLD are unable to attain the degree of understanding about the physical world that is necessary for them to achieve academically.

The implications of profound, complex disability, are therefore considerably more than just having to provide sensory cues to assist in these pupils accessing the National Curriculum. To consider the development of sensory function as representing one step at the bottom of a hierarchical framework of National Curriculum P levels is tokenistic. The status of sensory function would be degraded by such an act, and evidence of lateral learning within sensory function would be de-valued. The assessment framework of the National Curriculum is designed to celebrate the attainment of linear learning. The reporting of lateral learning within sensory function would have little value in the league-table mentality of the enterprise culture, and certainly would not further the social inclusion of pupils with profound disabilities.

The teaching of profoundly disabled pupils is undertaken at a sensory-function level with the intention of promoting emotional security and basic interaction (Nind and Hewett 1998). It is not unusual, however, for the teaching of these pupils to take place in circumstances that are contrary to those required for the promotion of effective learning. A school environment is often internally inconsistent, and the unpredictability of classroom events can be startling and disorientating for pupils with PMLD. Quite apart from these more unfortunate features of the typical school environment, profoundly disabled pupils are far more likely than their non-disabled peers to be in severe pain, have undetected illnesses, suffer from epilepsy, be at risk from pressure sores, and be severely underweight (Ganesh *et al.* 1994, Hutchinson 1998). All these factors need to be considered when the curriculum for pupils with PMLD is being planned.

As early as 1979, the complex characteristics of profoundly disabled pupils were being described as requiring close collaboration between teachers, doctors, psychologists, nurses and therapists (Warnock DES 1978). Multi-agency collaboration was considered essential for developing individual programmes with which to elicit the slightest of responses from profoundly disabled pupils. It is curious that recognition of these elaborate setting conditions has never enjoyed high status when the performance of SLD schools has been appraised. Although advice has been offered to suggest that curriculum planning for pupils with PMLD should be based upon individual need (SCAA 1996b), there is precious little evidence that such advice has ever been properly carried over into the framework for inspecting SLD schools.

The consultation document mentioned right at the start of this section, namely *Curriculum Guidelines for Pupils Attaining Significantly Below Age-Related Expectation* (Tilstone *et al.* 2000) paid some attention to the very subtle learning stages of:

- encounter;
- awareness;
- response;
- engagement;
- participation;
- involvement;
- attainment.

Some authors have described these stages as being typical of the behaviour shown by pupils with profound disabilities (Aitken and Buultjens 1992; Brown 1996), but scant attention was directed in the consultation document towards the pedagogy inherent within these alleged stages of learning. Profoundly disabled pupils have personal learning styles that are unlikely to alter dramatically through their school career, unless they have a regressive condition. The stages of learning that are typical of these pupils, as described above, are not linear in the sense that a pupil is ever able to demonstrate mastery of any particular stage and then move on to increasingly sophisticated stages of learning. These stages are only relevant in a *lateral* sense, and they are likely to apply to every learning experience throughout a pupil's school career. They may be used to help shape the curriculum experiences that are being offered to an individual pupil, but have little value for reporting attainment in an academic sense. They are useful only for noting when a pupil is beginning to make some sense of what is being taught, and for indicating that the setting conditions organised by the school staff are appropriate to the personal learning style of the pupil under instruction.

In Chapter 2, I described how the content of a generic prompt sheet could be used to help establish the personal learning styles of pupils with SLD/PMLD (Figure 2.1). Although the prompts contained in Figure 2.1 are not claimed to be definitive, their use can provide staff with sufficient information so as to organise appropriate setting conditions for engaging pupils in the process of learning. Consideration of the findings from Exercise 1, applied on a whole-school basis, could also provide an SLD school with a good indication of what needs to be included within the core curriculum.

Included within the personal learning styles of many pupils will be descriptions of the therapies and treatments that these pupils require in response to their innate disabilities. The place of therapies and treatments within the whole curriculum for profoundly disabled pupils has long been acknowledged (Warnock 1978; NCC 1992), but the actual delivery of these regimes can sometimes be considered a 'bolt on' to the curriculum – and even, perhaps, something that should not be allowed to take up too much of a pupil's taught day. The provision of therapies and medical treatments needs to be considered as a pupil's fundamental right, much more so than their right to the National Curriculum, and should therefore have a rightful place at the core of the SLD curriculum.

There may be some practitioners who argue that therapies and medical treatments have no place within the school day and that, in an ideal world, the delivery of such treatments should be undertaken in a pupil's home. Such conceited and ill-advised opinions fail to recognise that the needs of pupils with SLD/PMLD have to remain central to all aspects of school provision. It must not be assumed that therapies and medical treatments can be neatly packaged for delivery in isolation from a pupil's time at school. Provision for pupils with SLD/PMLD needs to be considered holistically if their education is ever going to be truly effective.

Not all the reasons why pupils with SLD/PMLD fail to develop along generalised patterns of child development can be simply attributed to circumstances that are 'within the child'. The school environment has a crucial role to play in how well these pupils are empowered to counter the handicapping effects of their impaired abilities. Teaching and caring for children with profound disabilities can, at times, be difficult and unrewarding for adults because of the lack of feedback that such children give in return (Ware 1996). When adults experience these kinds of feelings, they tend to reduce the rate and extent of their interaction with such children. The consequence is that some profoundly disabled children experience lack of security, stimulation, love and communication, which in turn reduces the likelihood of them seeking to interact with the outside world (Nind and Hewitt 1998). This unfortunate relationship serves to handicap some children beyond what can be accounted for as a consequence of their disability (Morris 1995).

Ensuring that information about a pupil's holistic needs are at the centre of what is taught in the SLD school is essential for providing the kind of school environment needed to promote effective staff/adult interaction. The need to combine findings from neurological examinations, observations of functional behaviour, and assessments of physiological and psychological function is absolutely essential if staff are to understand, and be able to empathise with, a pupil's abilities, needs and preferences (Porter *et al.* 1997). All of this needs to be reflected when seeking to define a meaningful curriculum for pupils with SLD/PMLD. Placing the personal learning styles of pupils at the core of such a curriculum is the point at which we need to start (see Figure 4.2).

A curriculum for holistic development

Pupils with SLD/PMLD have difficulty in interacting with their environment, a situation that can inhibit – or in some cases prohibit – their ability to learn and develop an understanding of the world around them. These difficulties may not simply be the result of a severe learning delay but can often be associated with complex psychiatric, neurological, psychological and physiological impairments, any of which can have an impact upon aspects of a pupil's functioning.

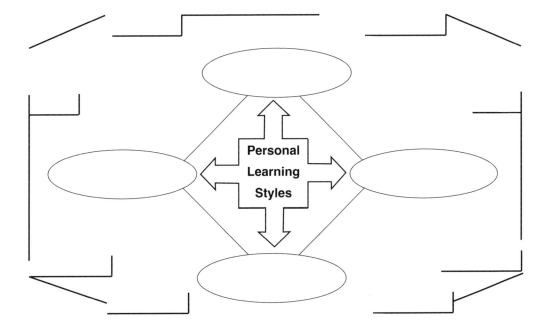

Figure 4.2 Keeping personal learning styles at the core of the curriculum

The extent to which such impairments become manifested in the characteristics of individual pupils will vary. For instance, the impact of a disability upon one pupil's behaviour may be restricted to an inability to concentrate, while for another pupil the impact may be profound, resulting in distressing characteristics such as severe, obsessive, self-injurious behaviour or life-limiting illness. The identification and treatment of these characteristics is often undertaken outside the immediate school environment, perhaps by a clinical psychologist, psychiatrist and/or other health professional, in isolation from the provision being made within school. In circumstances such as these, it is very difficult for school staff to recognise and respond to a pupil's individual characteristics without support from other agencies (Lacey 1998), and multi-agency collaboration will be essential for the design and delivery of an effective curriculum.

A recent example of good multi-agency collaboration, in response to the implications of disability, may be seen in work undertaken in Coventry with pupils with SLD who had an additional diagnosis of ASD (Aird and Lister 1999). An increasing number of pupils being diagnosed with ASD, together with the high profile of ASD in local SEN tribunals, helped focus attention upon the need to take special note of the personal learning styles of pupils with ASD. Multi-agency collaboration was undertaken with the intention of ensuring that the education of these pupils would be focused upon their individual needs and particularly upon the development of their inter-personal communication skills, social empathy and emotional stability.

Information from the personal learning styles of pupils with ASD was used for developing specialist curricula to be placed at the core of the Coventry school's whole curriculum. Monitoring the progress of pupils was undertaken by different agencies working in collaboration, directed partly at the linear progress that pupils were making within specialist curricula and partly at noting subtle changes within the personal learning styles of pupils, which was felt to represent pupil progress in a more lateral sense. Monitoring the linear progress of pupils helped to demonstrate that pupils were making progress in the areas of knowledge, skill and understanding relating to the triad of impairment (Wing 1996). Monitoring lateral progress within the personal learning styles of pupils helped ensure that the setting conditions for these pupils were being applied consistently across the timetable in order to minimise the disabling effects of ASD.

Inevitably, there are examples of poor curriculum planning in response to the personal learning styles of pupils with SLD/PMLD. Some of the poorest of these can be readily observed in the use and abuse of 'high tech' sensory rooms, with pupils often referred to as 'hard to reach'. In the worst examples, pupils are to be found propped in front of bubble tubes and an assortment of florescent, vibrating electronic gadgets in a vague belief that they may learn to be less hard to reach and even, perhaps, learn something about early concepts of the National Curriculum via a mysterious process of sensory osmosis. In better examples, the sensory function of pupils will have been accurately assessed, and pupils engaged in specialist curricula that have been designed to promote sensory and perceptual develop-ment, via teaching methodologies that take pupil preference into account and that are supported by resources specifically selected for the task in hand.

It ought not to be assumed that a profoundly disabled pupil will use his or her residual senses as non-disabled pupils do, and neither should it be assumed that the best way forward for teaching such a pupil will be by reference to some gener-alised pattern of sensory development. Although it is certainly possible and considered good practice for SLD schools to develop specialist curricula in response to the personal learning styles of profoundly disabled pupils (see Chapter 5 for a discussion of this topic), it is usually the case that the curriculum needs to begin with the quintessential needs of individual pupils. Rather than subject a pupil to a battery of sensory stimulants in the hope of striking lucky, a better starting point would be to begin with the pupil's personal learning style and provide a safe, secure and predictable learning environment into which sensory stimuli may be introduced gradually, their impact upon the pupil's personal learning style noted, and elements of good practice disseminated across the timetable into subjects of the core and peripheral curricula.

When a pupil's personal learning style can be readily identified and used in a formative way to create a more interactive and effective learning environment, staff are generally quick to value this information as being central to their teaching style and as being at the core of what the pupil needs to learn about. Conversely, when the idiosyncratic needs of pupils are not given a high status within whole-school management, or are relegated to P level status situated at the bottom rung of the National Curriculum ladder, staff are unlikely to value the importance of personal learning styles. In an educational climate where every minute of the timetable is crammed to overflowing and where subjects of the National Curriculum are often expected to be given priority, who can blame staff for not fully appreciating the importance of keeping the personal learning styles of each pupil central to their teaching.

There is considerable pressure upon teachers in SLD schools to be seen to be 'doing the National Curriculum', but teachers also need to bear in mind that they must draw from the whole curriculum in order to plan their teaching and ensure that their pupils are actively participating in activities, rather than just being present (SCAA 1996b). Subjects of the National Curriculum have been described as being valuable for providing stimulating contexts for experiential learning (Byers 1999) and techniques such as jigsawing (Johnson and Johnson 1987; Rose 1991) have proved helpful for giving advice about differentiation within lesson planning. However, there has been little advice published about the importance of establishing the appropriate setting conditions for effective learning to take place. Perhaps this absence has something to do with the rejection of the behaviourist philosophy that was fashionable during the 1970s and early 1980s. Or, perhaps, it has something to do with a fear of approaches that are more akin to medical models of treatment than they are to mainstream teaching methodologies. Whatever the reason, there has been a noticeable absence of advice concerned with the personal learning styles of pupils with SLD/PMLD at the core of the whole curriculum.

Academics within the field of SEN may argue that using personal learning styles as the starting point for the development of the whole curriculum confuses pedagogy – i.e., actions that are required in order to work co-actively with a pupil (MacFarland 1995; Porter *et al.* 1997) – with organisational strategies, such as the positioning of a pupil in response to a physical deformity. Such confusion is unavoidable, given the complex and idiosyncratic nature of the setting conditions that some pupils with SLD/PMLD require. Whether the information contained within personal learning styles relates to pedagogy and/or organisational strategy is largely irrelevant to a school's fundamental goal of empowering pupil performance within the whole curriculum. Pupils with SLD/PMLD require particular setting conditions in order to learn effectively, and the only way to facilitate such an enabling environment is by keeping personal learning styles at the core of everything that SLD schools wish to teach.

CHAPTER 5

Specialist curricula at the core of the curriculum

Demise and fragmentation of the traditional specialist SLD curriculum

Writing in 1992, the National Curriculum Council (NCC) advised that, for pupils with SLD/PMLD, access to the National Curriculum alone would not be able to meet all of their needs, and that, furthermore, additional subjects beyond those of the National Curriculum, would be required in order for a school's whole curriculum to address these shortfalls (NCC 1992). There was no indication that the National Curriculum was intended to replace the specialist curricula that many SLD schools had developed prior to ERA88. The NCC was keen to assure teachers that the National Curriculum was intended to build upon existing practice, and it went so far as to publish a statement to that effect (NCC 1992). Additional advice followed, to reinforce that view (SCAA 1996b).

This advice regarding the National Curriculum reminded teachers in SLD schools that the whole curriculum for pupils with PMLD was greater than the National Curriculum. The SCAA urged SLD schools not to become anxious about the matter of allocating specific hours to the teaching of individual subjects of the National Curriculum, but to be guided instead by considering how teaching time could be most profitably used to ensure a productive learning environment (SCAA 1996b). Flexibility was described as the key for securing an appropriate balance within the whole curriculum. Teachers were advised to divide their time between enabling the entitlement of their pupils to access the National Curriculum and teaching additional curricula in response to specific pupil need (SCAA 1996b).

This common-sense approach to curriculum delivery was unfortunately never in evidence within the OFSTED inspection framework for SLD schools, and the appraisal of additional specialist curricula was not afforded any status in the

1994–1998 review of inspection findings at the end of the first round of special-school inspections (OFSTED 1998). The focus of these inspections remained instead firmly upon teaching and achievement within the National Curriculum. This failure to provide an adequate system for appraising the *whole* curriculum in SLD schools undoubtedly contributed to the demise of the traditional SLD curriculum. Although sensible advice was being expressed by the NCC and SCAA about the design of the whole curriculum in SLD schools, the profound ambiguities experienced during OFSTED inspections were sufficient for SLD schools to turn away from their traditional specialist curriculum and adapt their practice to better suit the demands of the National Curriculum.

New guidance about the teaching of Personal, Social and Health Education (PSHE) and Citizenship at Key Stages 3 and 4 was introduced at the end of the 1990s (QCA, 2000a, 2000b). These additional subjects were added to the National Curriculum in order that society would benefit from pupils who were healthier, more active and more confident in their role in the community (QCA 2000a). The spirit of this guidance has much in common with the traditional ethos of SLD schools and, in places, the actual content of these new subjects partly overlaps with aspects of the traditional specialist SLD curriculum. However, it remains to be seen whether the opportunity afforded by the new advice on the teaching of PSHE and Citizenship will assist SLD schools in re-establishing their traditional values, or merely serve to confuse matters further. The overlaps in content between these new subjects and the traditional SLD curriculum is more by chance than by design. The guidance lacks any insight into the ways in which profound disability inhibits the social inclusion of pupils with SLD/PMLD, and implementation of this new guidance may unfortunately result in further fragmentation of traditional SLD practice.

It was not surprising that the survey of provision for pupils with MSI, undertaken in 1997, found that, although teachers in special schools advocated the need for additional specialist curricula, the actual provision of such specialist curricula was rarely evident in practice (Porter *et al.* 1997). Findings from this survey showed fragmentation and inconsistency in the provision of specialist curricula for pupils with profound and complex impairments. Although the hijacking of specialist curricula in order to shore up a fundamentally flawed National Curriculum – as typified by the development of P levels, PSHE and Citizenship – will help to strengthen societal control of SLD school practice, it is unlikely to provide a logical and coherent way forward for the development of an effective whole curriculum for pupils with SLD/PMLD. It is worth remembering that the traditional specialist SLD curriculum was developed specifically to respond to the implications of profound disability and not with the intention of allowing access by disabled pupils to the mainstream curriculum. To try and re-label aspects of the traditional SLD curriculum in order to better suit the demands of the National Curriculum marks an unfortunate return to the re-description strategies of the early 1990s, which were firmly condemned at the time as an 'elaborate pretence' (Byers 1999).

The specialist curriculum

Of particular interest was the work being undertaken to develop a philosophical basis for the development of the whole curriculum in SLD schools. Marlett writing in 1984, identified four major influences which were believed to represent a fundamental basis for defining the whole curriculum for pupils with SLD/PMLD (Fagg *et al.* 1990).

- adaptive influences (teaching based upon medical models of intervention, in direct response to physical and sensory impairments);
- developmental influences (teaching to help pupils achieve developmental and behavioural milestones);
- behavioural influences (teaching that uses finely graded learning steps to help pupils develop specific skills and/or understandings);
- functional influences (teaching practical/vocational skills in realistic settings).

This current chapter seeks to describe ways in which Marlett's four influences can be brought together when defining the content of the core curriculum for pupils with SLD/PMLD (see Figure 5.1).

It is possible to address some of the educational, care and treatment implications of an individual pupil's disability by ensuring that personal learning styles are used to shape everyday provision. However, there will always be some special needs that require the provision of additional, specialist curricula in order for the handicapping effects of disability to be minimised. Although medical treatments and therapies are an intrinsic part of a specialist curriculum, such a curriculum needs to extend considerably beyond paramedical provision. The implications of profound disability are far-reaching and they impact upon many aspects of basic functioning. People with SLD/PMLD need proper support if they are to participate as actively as is possible within society (Sanderson *et al.* 1997). The provision of specialist curricula can do much to provide this support and thus enable pupils with SLD/PMLD to participate more effectively within their community than would otherwise be the case.

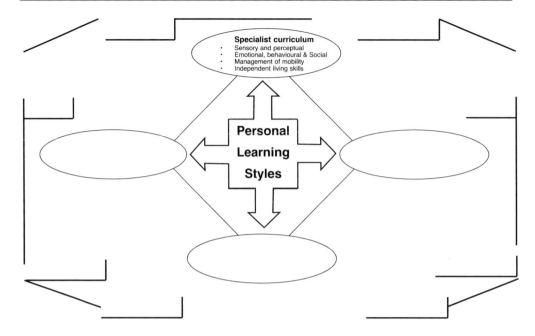

Figure 5.1 Specialist curricula at the core of the curriculum

Four additional, specialist curriculum areas are recommended for inclusion at the core of the whole curriculum for the SLD school, the first two of which are described in further detail below. The four areas are:

- sensory and perceptual education;
- emotional, behavioural and social education;
- management of mobility;
- independent living skills and self-determination.

The titles that a school grants to components within its specialist curriculum are somewhat arbitrary, but for the sake of clarity and coherence, it is best that the titles, as well as the content, have obvious links with the kinds of impairments typical of pupils with SLD/PMLD, and that they seek to reflect the kinds of influences described by Marlett.

Sensory and perceptual education

The incidence of sensory impairment in pupils with SLD/PMLD is far greater than the norm and is particularly so in profoundly disabled pupils (Ouvry 1987). The distance senses have particular importance for enabling children to learn effectively (Warren 1994; Rosen 1997), and so it can only be deemed sensible for

SLD schools to pay special attention to enabling their pupils to develop effective sensory function. Although it is not uncommon to hear staff in SLD schools discussing the importance of providing a sensory curriculum for their pupils, there is a worrying absence of good practice in the teaching of sensory function in these types of school (Porter *et al.* 1997).

It may be that understanding of the content and design of a sensory curriculum for pupils with SLD/PMLD has become confused. Since the introduction of the National Curriculum, sensory function has tended to be associated with the practical need to provide some disabled pupils with sensory clues with which to help them access concepts relating to P levels, and/or to provide teachers with functional strategies for differentiating their lesson plans. From a functional perspective, sensory clues are important for helping some disabled pupils access new concepts, but it is vital that sensory-based teaching approaches are properly aided by the findings of medical diagnosis and the formative assessment of the sensory and perceptual abilities of the pupils under instruction. Teaching strategies need to be firmly based on the adaptive and developmental perspectives of sensory and perceptual impairment if there are to be any functional and behavioural benefits gained from the use of sensory clues within everyday, cross-curricular lesson planning. The demise of initial specialist training for teachers in SLD schools will, no doubt, have contributed to the poor showing of sensory-function teaching in SLD schools during the 1997 survey of the provision for pupils with MSI.

It is sometimes claimed that the use of a Multi-Sensory Environment (MSE) is useful for teaching pupils with PMLD and for promoting their curriculum access. The types of skill that it is sometimes claimed can be taught effectively by the use of an MSE range from decision making through switch operation to colour matching (Porter and Miller 2000). The important place of MSEs in the SLD school is now well established and it is not unusual to find the use of an MSE room as a timetabled subject in its own right in some schools (Porter and Miller 2000). In the absence of a well-informed sensory curriculum, there is a risk that use of an MSE facility may become an end in itself for some 'hard to reach' pupils; or, alternatively, the MSE becomes relegated to the status of an expensive leisure and relaxation facility (Orr 2000). It is worth remembering that MSEs tend to be designed and promoted by commercial companies who sell the equipment (as are many of the training courses on use of an MSE). The promotion of MSEs tends to be resource-led, as opposed to curriculum led, because the sale of equipment is usually the predominant concern of the companies who advertise and organise MSE training events

A good number of pupils in SLD schools, particularly pupils with PMLD, exhibit sensory impairments that are of an idiosyncratic nature and for whom medical interventions and adaptive corrective treatments are not always relevant. Good examples of these types of sensory impairment are represented by instances of cortical blindness and/or central deafness. In cortical blindness, the mechanisms of the eye are intact but the brain, for whatever reason, is unable to make any sense of the visual information being received. Likewise, for the pupil with central deafness, the mechanisms of the ear function well enough but the pupil is unable to make sense of any auditory information that the ear may be detecting. For pupils with such disabilities, the opportunity to develop their sensory and perceptual abilities is of huge importance; and in the absence of medical treatment, school staff need to fall back on the support of a specialist curriculum, which can help the diagnostic process and also provide useful teaching strategies (Pagliano 1999).

A specialist curriculum is required that can bring together medically biased adaptive treatments with teaching strategies that are of a developmental, behavioural and functional nature. The assessment framework of such a curriculum needs to be sufficiently detailed so as to build upon the findings of a medical diagnosis and enable a formative assessment of a pupil's sensory and perceptual abilities to be undertaken. It should only be after such a specialist curriculum has been developed, in collaboration with specialist support services, that the design of MSEs and the purchase of specialist resources should be undertaken. Likewise, the use of sensory teaching approaches to help pupils access subjects of the National Curriculum should only be undertaken after a pupil has benefited from a thorough, multi-agency assessment and a coherent teaching strategy has been agreed.

Emotional, behavioural and social education

Many pupils with SLD/PMLD display severe challenging behaviour. The reasons why so many of these pupils display such behaviour varies, and it may often be associated with catalysts such as impaired communication, the implications of ASD, temporal lobe epilepsy and undiagnosed pain. Recent estimates suggest that 8 per cent of pupils in an average SLD school will have severe challenging behaviour, while another 12 per cent will have challenging behaviour of a lesser nature (Kiernan and Kiernan 1994).

Working with pupils with severe challenging behaviour imposes great pressures upon staff (Male and May 1997a, 1997b), and when a school community is threatened by a pupil with overtly violent behaviour, it is often expected that a school's SMT will resort to robust measures to either contain or remove the pupil's immediate threat of physical injury (NUT 2000). Overt violent behaviour tends to be considered as something that is within the child and that requires medical or clinical treatments. The management of pupils with severe challenging behaviour poses SLD schools with something of a dilemma. There are serious ethical dilemmas, relating to the use of physical restraint, pharmaceutical treatments and behaviour-modification programmes, which all need to be considered if pupils with severe challenging behaviour are to enjoy 'ordinary life' rights as expressed in the United Nations' *Convention on the Rights of the Child* (1989).

Although there may well be a pragmatic basis for containing or removing a pupil's overt violent behaviour, staff need to understand the developmental and functional reasons why some pupils behave aggressively and how these pupils can be taught to reduce their need to resort to violent behaviour (Harris 1996). Without the benefit of a specialist curriculum to assist staff in understanding and responding to occasions of severe challenging behaviour, containment or exclusion are the only strategies remaining. Neither of these two strategies enables the social inclusion of pupils with severe challenging behaviour, and in some quarters there are growing concerns about the shortcomings in provision for pupils who have a learning difficulty and severe challenging behaviour (Russell 1997). For example, an increasing emphasis upon structured teaching in special schools, associated with implementation of the National Curriculum, has been reported as being of particular concern (Mental Health Foundation 1997).

Pupils with severe challenging behaviour lack the kinds of developmental and functional skills that are essential for their social inclusion (Kiernan and Kiernan 1994; Harris 1996). The curriculum implications associated with these needs go far beyond the scope of the newly revised cross-curricular subjects of PSHE and Citizenship (DfEE 2000a, 2000b). A specialist curriculum is required that brings together the teaching of functional emotional, behavioural and social skills with the provision of developmental, behavioural and adaptive clinical treatments.

Additional subjects of the specialist curriculum

There is insufficient space within this book to set out all the arguments in support of developing specialist curricula at the core of the SLD curriculum. The arguments that have been used to support the development of specialist curricula for sensory and perceptual development, and also of emotional, behavioural and social development, are intended to demonstrate the kinds of existing knowledge that can be used by an SLD school to defend the development of a specialist curriculum that is additional to the National Curriculum.

Two other areas that SLD schools might wish to address include motor development, and independent living skills, for there is a wealth of published material to support the need for them. For example, Hogg (1986) clearly defended the need for a curriculum with a high motoric component for pupils with SLD/PMLD by considering the findings of research into the motor deficits typical of pupils with learning difficulties, undertaken by Hogg (1982) and Henderson (1985). There is a need for a specialist curriculum that can bring together the adaptive medical treatments of physical disability with the teaching of functional motor skills across a whole curriculum. There are similar arguments to support the need to teach pupils with SLD/PMLD specific skills that can aid their opportunities for social inclusion. Such skills range from basic self-help skills, such as dressing and personal hygiene, to more subtle skills such as self-advocacy and self-determination.

There is a powerful and urgent need for SLD schools to re-invoke the status of their specialist curricula and ensure that the educational implications of disability can be properly addressed within the organisation of the whole curriculum. Although adoption of the personal learning style strategy could enable an SLD school to ensure that teaching and caring methods are empathetic to the behaviour of their individual pupils, these pupils require specialist teaching in order to make progress in a functional and developmental sense. Linking the selection and management of IEP (Individual Education Plan) targets to a coherent and well-organised specialist curriculum, at the core of the SLD curriculum, would enable pupils to make progress within the areas of function and/or development where they have in the greatest need.

Designing a specialist curriculum

In terms of practical design for a specialist curriculum, it is suggested that each of the subjects adopted for inclusion within the specialist curriculum should have a consistent format and ought to include as a minimum:

- a set of assessment criteria to help identify the educational implications of a pupil's diagnosis within a specific area of disability;
- sets of teaching activities that correspond to each assessment criterion, designed to teach the skills and concepts relevant to a pupil's specific area of need;
- a monitoring pro forma with which to record progress.

Some suggestions as to what might be included as principal areas within each subject of the specialist curriculum have been provided in Figure 5.2. However, the actual content will need to be agreed by a school's staff, working in collaboration with supporting professionals who are knowledgeable in the areas under consideration. As a consequence of collaborative planning, the resulting specialist curriculum would bring together adaptive, developmental, behavioural and functional considerations.

Because of the limitations of space in this publication, exemplar material is provided for just one of the subjects recommended for inclusion within the specialist curriculum. This exemplar material relates to the suggested curriculum for emotional, behavioural and social education.

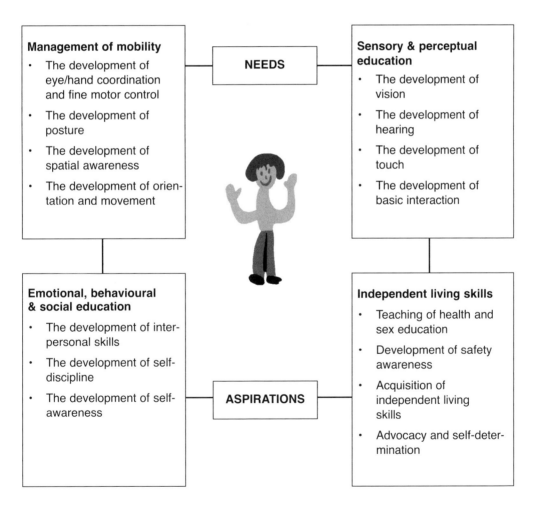

Figure 5.2 Principal areas within subjects of the specialist curriculum

The specialist curriculum for emotional, behavioural and social education: an example

A number of pupils with SLD/PMLD behave in ways that are considered inappropriate for enabling their social inclusion. For some pupils, the intensity of their inappropriate behaviour is extreme and can be severely challenging to those who educate and care for them. For the most part, specialist provision that has been developed in response to these emotional, behavioural and social difficulties has been based upon the use of tried and tested behaviour modification techniques, such as those disseminated via the *Education of the Developmentally Young Children* package (Foxen and McBrien 1981). Where collaborative working has been possible, SLD schools have also developed partnership working with health authority staff such as psychiatrists, clinical psychologists and community nurses, to help in the delivery of adaptive treatment regimes. Provision has largely focused upon treating or adapting a pupil's problem behaviour, so as to improve their opportunities for social inclusion.

An unfortunate aspect of much of this specialist provision is that the treatment provided often has little to do with resolving the reasons why a particular pupil is behaving inappropriately. Modification programmes, physical-restraint techniques and medication regimes may all help to treat the symptoms of challenging behaviour but they are not always effective in empowering the pupil in question to develop the skills and abilities necessary for them to cope with the demands of society. Research into the behaviour of pupils with SLD/PMLD has demonstrated that these pupils are likely to have a variety of reasons for behaving inappropriately, including (adapted from Harris *et al.* 1996):

- an inability to communicate basic needs;
- limited social experiences;
- irrational, intrusive phobias;
- limited language and lack of understanding;
- ritualistic, intrusive behaviours;
- intolerance of overstimulation;
- undetected illness and injury;
- a high incidence of mental illness;
- syndromes with associated behavioural dysfunction;
- high levels of discomfort from incontinence and/or physical impairment;
- a low boredom threshold;
- emotional insecurity as a result of a sensory impairment.

The sheer diversity of reasons for pupils with SLD/PMLD behaving as they do means that it is not possible to rely on one or two treatment strategies (Smith 1991). What is required is a combination of strategies. Figure 5.3 illustrates the combination of strategies that an SLD school should consider when responding to the needs of pupils who have emotional, behavioural and social difficulties.

Pharmaceutical interventions, behavioural teaching techniques and environmental interventions are all considerations that should be agreed, via multi-agency collaboration, for inclusion within a pupil's personal learning style. These are the kinds of practical arrangements that need to be implemented consistently in order to control a pupil's behaviour and begin to enable their inclusion within the school community. However, in order properly to enable the social inclusion of pupils with SLD/PMLD, it is also necessary to consider what skills these pupils require in order to cope with the demands of society. If a school deems it necessary to intervene in the way some pupils behave, by imposing behaviour modification techniques or medication regimes and/or by modifying the learning environment, then it should also be deemed necessary to ensure that the school's curriculum reflects such a high-priority need.

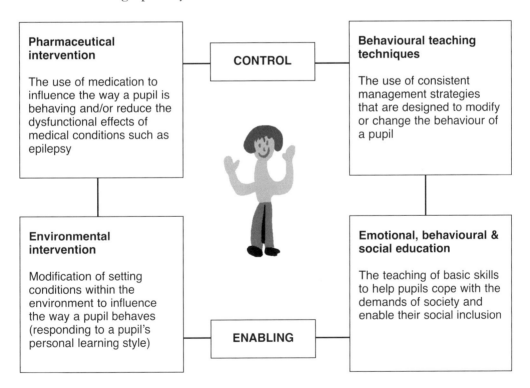

Figure 5.3 Strategies for managing pupils with emotional, behavioural and social difficulties

Activities within everyday lessons can be used to promote social inclusion skills in a general way on behalf of all pupils. For instance, a school might decide that all Physical Education lessons should include focuses on:

- self-image – ice-breaking games that are intended to reinforce body image and self-awareness;
- working in pairs – games that are intended to develop one-to-one interactions (such as eye contact), build up mutual trust and reduce tactile defensiveness;
- working in a group – games that are intended to promote social empathy, cooperation and coping with the stress of group dynamics.

A clearly identified structure to lessons can in this way provide useful opportunities for helping pupils rehearse their social-inclusion skills.

However, simply providing these kinds of opportunities is insufficient for the needs of pupils who have more severe behavioural difficulties, and this is where a specialist curriculum for emotional, behavioural and social education can prove to be so valuable. Figure 5.4 includes suggestions for the content of such a curriculum, which is intended to help pupils develop important social-inclusion skills, such as:

- relating to others;
- expressing an opinion;
- coping with stress;
- trusting others;
- coping with anger;
- making decisions;
- coping with responsibility.

Specialist curricula relating to the development of interpersonal skills

As illustrated in Figure 5.4, a curriculum for emotional, behavioural and social education can be divided into three major components. Although there will inevitably be areas where the content of these components overlap, dividing the subject matter in this way assists in the assessment of a pupil's needs within the subject and in the subsequent monitoring of pupil progress.

Determination of the actual content of each component is variable, and a school's staff should work in consultation with colleagues from supporting agencies in order to define the types of skills and abilities that are felt to be prerequisite for securing effective social inclusion. There are numerous books on the

The development of inter-personal skills
- Relating to others
- Showing empathy
- Cooperating with others
- Trusting a partner
- Understanding emotions
- Making decisions
- Understanding the meaning of friendship
- Communicating feelings

The development of self-awareness
- Having a positive self-image
- Advocating likes and dislikes
- Coping with emotions
- Sharing personal items with others
- Acknowledging different aspects of one's own behaviour

The development of self-discipline
- Coping with anger
- Recognising rules and responsibilities
- Controlling sexual feelings
- Demonstrating assertiveness and self-determination
- Resolving conflicts
- Staying on task

Figure 5.4 Content of a curriculum for emotional, behavioural and social education

market that describe all manner of activities that can be easily adapted for inclusion in an emerging specialist curriculum for emotional, behavioural and social education.

Figure 5.5 suggests what assessment criteria might be relevant to the development of interpersonal skills (coded INP1–INP6). The assessment criteria have been coded so that corresponding sets of teaching activities can be developed. In the example of Figure 5.5, a pupil's priority need has been agreed as INP1 and a corresponding set of teaching activities has been selected from the associated curriculum material for use in the classroom with a small group of pupils.

This brief example serves to illustrate how easily a specialist curriculum can be developed in response to the emotional, behavioural and social needs of pupils on roll. Once the principal skill areas have been agreed, collaborative work can readily identify the framework of assessment criteria that will define the curriculum for social inclusion. The remaining task of collating sets of teaching activities, to correspond with the coded assessment framework, is a relatively straightforward one and can be readily undertaken by small teams of staff. This team approach helps in the dissemination, ownership and appreciation of the value of the specialist subject matter.

A Curriculum for Emotional, Behavioural & Social Education
Assessment and diagnostic criteria for the development of inter-personal skills

INP1 Cooperating with others
INP2 Trusting a partner
INP3 Understanding emotions
INP4 Making decisions
INP5 Understanding the meaning of friendship
INP6 Communicating feelings

A Curriculum for Emotional, Behavioural & Social Education
Curriculum materials for the development of inter-personal skills (INP)

INP1 : Cooperating with others

NP1.1 Using elastic rings co-actively

Note: This is a simple, fun activity for keeping even reasonably hyperactive pupils within a group because the feel of the elastic ring is often sufficient to keep their interest as the ring itself provides a natural boundary. The use of the ring enables pupils who are reluctant to engage in inter-personal activities, e.g., those who find holding hands threatening, to work co-actively with a partner and develop cooperation skills by physically mirroring their neighbour's actions.

Resources required:
Large elastic ring with a diameter of around 1.5 metres

Activity:
Pupils should be seated in a circle with the elastic ring stretched around the outside of the circle so that it is reasonably firm against the backs of pupils. Pupils grasp the ring in both hands and each pupil in turn is prompted to use small pulling, pushing, raising and lowering movements to stretch the elastic. Neighbouring pupils are encouraged to try and feel the movements and then copy the actions and so pass the activity around members of the group.

 As pupils develop a sense of confidence whilst performing their individual movements, group activities can be introduced by prompting pupils to move the ring around the circle by pulling it one way and then another. Rhymes and songs can be used to help provide verbal prompts and the rate at which the ring is moved around the circle can be varied. (Adapted from Jabadao, Leeds.)

NP1.2 Using elastic rings for name games

Resources required:
Large elastic ring with a diameter of around 1.5 metres
Large soft ball

Activity:
Pupils are seated in a circle holding the ring with both hands and with their legs apart. One pupil is selected to let go of the ring and to roll a ball towards another member of the group. The teacher can decide the name of the pupil to whom the ball is to be rolled towards or the pupil asked to make a choice.

Figure 5.5 Example of how specialist curricula for Emotional, Behavioural & Social Education can be used in the classroom

The process that has been described for the development of emotional, behavioural and social education can be replicated for any other subjects a school might choose to include within its specialist curriculum, such as those already listed in Chapter 4:

- sensory and perceptual education;
- the management of mobility;
- independent living skills.

Once a school's specialist curriculum is complete, the needs of individual pupils may be determined by considering their abilities against the assessment criteria of each subject. Where it is identified that a pupil has particular weaknesses, the relevant criteria are used to help decide targets within the pupil's IEP. When IEP targets are based upon the assessment criteria of the specialist curriculum in this way, it is a simple matter to use the corresponding teaching activities in response to a pupil's special needs.

Progress within IEP targets may be monitored by appraising pupil performance during teaching activities that have been specifically designed to promote the skills or concepts under consideration. When this process is applied across all subjects of a specialist curriculum, it ensures that there are tangible links established between the management of an individual pupil's IEP targets and the provision of teaching and learning. When, furthermore, required resources are identified within the framework of the specialist curriculum, it also helps to ensure good value for money.

Concluding comment

The whole curriculum for pupils with SLD/PMLD should be one that is flexible and that contains additional specialist curricula that are responsive to individual pupil need (SCAA 1996b). The time has come for SLD schools finally to respond to the SCAA's sensible advice and place specialist curricula at the core of the whole curriculum. However, it is vital that this specialist curriculum is designed with the needs of disabled pupils foremost in people's minds and is not made up of confused and confusing fragments of the National Curriculum. Placing specialist curricula at the core of the whole curriculum is another important step towards securing clarity of purpose for the SLD school.

CHAPTER 6

Conventional subjects in the core and peripheral curriculum

Throughout the past decade, SLD schools – the same as all other schools in the country – have been subject to a plethora of change. Since the landmark legislation of ERA88, successive governments have implemented educational reform after educational reform, targeted mainly on raising standards in academic achievement. Although the bulk of educational reform has been concerned with the raising of standards in mainstream schools, the demands for change have extended to include all sectors of education, including the SLD sector. Unfortunately, the needs, rights and aspirations of pupils with SLD/PMLD have not often been at the forefront of the thinking for this.

Because the circumstances of pupils with SLD/PMLD have not been properly considered when educational reforms have been introduced, SLD schools have had to implement changes that have not always been to the obvious benefit of their pupils. For example, since the implementation of LMS and the introduction of the National Curriculum, there has been an increase in the number of profoundly disabled pupils being socially excluded (Department of Health and Social Services Inspectorate 1993), and school life has been reported as becoming increasingly difficult for pupils with SLD and severe challenging behaviour (Mental Health Foundation 1997).

Although extensive comment has been made about the importance of considering the needs of pupils with SLD/PMLD at the time when educational reforms are being developed, there has been little evidence of this in practice. *The National Literacy Strategy* (DfEE 1998d), for example, was developed without any consideration of the needs of pupils with SLD/PMLD, and SLD schools were left trying to interpret what the implications of teaching literacy might be for their pupils (Aird 2000b). Also, when the National Framework for Teaching Mathematics (DfEE 1999b) was being piloted, no special schools were invited to join the first cohort to undertake the scheme and, as with the development of the Literacy

Strategy, the Framework for Mathematics was developed without considering the needs of pupils with SLD/PMLD (Robbins 2000).

Increasingly over the past 10 years, SLD schools have been required to respond to demands that risk compromising the needs, rights and aspirations of their pupils. Demands for change have had an impact upon how schools are organised and what they are required to teach. Most recently, government demands have also impacted upon *how* schools should teach. Great clarity of vision is required to know how and what to teach pupils with SLD/PMLD, but the government has expected SLD schools to fall into line with educational reforms that have obviously not taken such pupils into consideration. The scale and manner in which changes have been imposed have resulted in what can only be described as 'tunnel vision' where the provision for pupils with SEN is concerned The fact that SEN provision nationally has failed to develop along any unified pattern (Sebba *et al.* 1996) is tangible evidence of this tunnel vision. The time has come for governors and head teachers to answer the question as to whether SLD schools exist in order to help disabled children to flourish or, alternatively, whether they exist merely in order to facilitate societal control (Sebba *et al.* 1995).

Clarity of purpose is the key to interpreting the needs, rights and aspirations of pupils with SLD/PMLD and the most powerful tool that SLD schools possess for enabling these needs, rights and aspirations to be met is that of the whole curriculum (Carpenter and Ashdown 1996). However, the pressure of external demands is now so great that SLD schools risk losing control over their curriculum. If SLD schools are ever going to re-establish this control, then a meaningful rationale for the whole curriculum is urgently required. That rationale needs to recognise the difficulties that exist when seeking to reduce subjects of the National Curriculum to levels that are relevant to the abilities of some pupils with SLD/PMLD. There are significant values to be gained from teaching subjects of the National Curriculum but the level of simplification that is required can often render the content of such teaching unrecognisable as belonging to any particular subject (Turner 2000). In addition to clarifying the rationale for placing specialist curricula at the core of the SLD curriculum, a similar exercise needs to be undertaken to clarify the rationale for organising the subjects within the National Curriculum into the core and peripheral curriculum of each SLD school.

There will always be differences of opinion expressed about the relative importance awarded to one subject, as compared to another. In an SLD school, in particular, there are likely to be disputes over the weighting awarded to subjects of the National Curriculum as compared with other parts of the whole curriculum (Sebba *et al.* 1995). The diagrams that are used in this book to illustrate the design of the whole curriculum provide a pictorial representation of suggested relative weightings awarded to different subjects. The figures place personal learning styles of individual pupils at the very centre of the whole curriculum. Radiating out from that centre are the various subjects that are suggested should form the core curriculum for the SLD school, followed by reference to subjects representing the peripheral curriculum.

English and Communication, Mathematics and Information and Communications Technology (ICT) in the core curriculum

The place of the specialist curriculum has already been discussed at length in Chapter 5. Some of the teaching within that specialist curriculum will need to be performed discretely for some pupils, closely related to the need for a school to address priority targets within its pupils' IEPs. Other specialist teaching may also be undertaken in a cross-curricular manner, to enable pupils to generalise their emerging abilities and assist them in accessing the broader entitlement curriculum.

However, the need to address the specific idiosyncratic implications of disability should not be considered as being the sole function of the core curriculum within the SLD school. Pupils with SLD/PMLD also have common needs, and it is recommended that the subjects of English, Mathematics and ICT need to feature as essential components within the core curriculum in response to these shared needs – as illustrated in Figure 6.1.

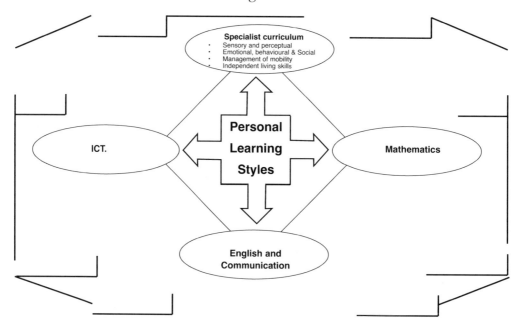

Figure 6:1 English and Communication, Mathematics and Information and Communications Technology (ICT) in the core curriculum

In order for pupils with SLD/PMLD to become effective learners, it is first necessary to minimise the handicapping affects of their specific disabilities so that their residual skills, abilities and behaviours, which are often prerequisite to effective learning, can be suitably developed. Secondly, in response to the global developmental delay that all pupils with SLD/PMLD display, these pupils require concentrated efforts to enable them to learn:

- how to communicate effectively;
- how to understand the basic principles that govern the complex world around them;
- how to exercise some degree of control over their environment in order to participate within it.

This simple rationale is the basis of an argument that advocates that the subjects of English and Communication, Mathematics and ICT are the most logical subjects with which to enable pupils with SLD/PMLD to become effective learners. Figure 6.2 serves to illustrate the reasons why these three subjects are considered to be essential within the core curriculum. These reasons revolve around the educational processes of:

- enabling;
- engaging;
- empowering;
- equipping.

In a volume of this size and scope, there is insufficient space to devote equal attention to each of these three conventional subjects. Suffice it to say that English and Communication has been given preferential treatment here. This is not intended to understate the place of Mathematics and ICT within the core curriculum, for these subjects are also discussed – to a lesser degree – later in the section; it is simply the belief that English has a more important place within the SLD curriculum.

The teaching of English and Communication

English enjoys special treatment within this text because of its intrinsic importance to the education of pupils with SLD/PMLD. It has a crucial role to play in the teaching of all pupils across the whole curriculum (SCAA 1997a) and for pupils with SLD/PMLD this important cross-curricular role is even more pronounced (Aird and Heath 2000).

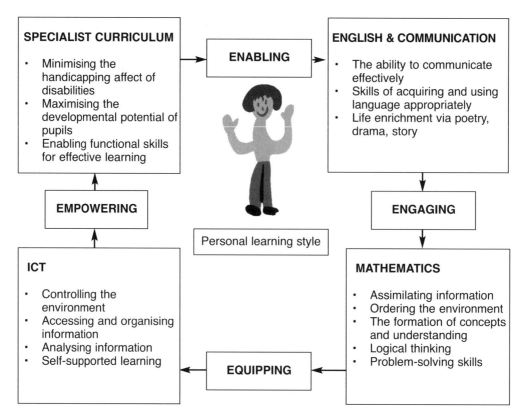

Figure 6.2 Rationale for the core curriculum

The way in which the majority of schools are expected to enable their pupils to learn relies heavily upon the ability of both teachers and pupils to have effective oral and written communication skills that they can apply across the whole curriculum (SCAA 1997a). However, pupils with SLD/PMLD have innate difficulties in their ability to communicate effectively through oral or written means. These difficulties exist partly as a consequence of impairments to their neurological, psychological and physiological functions, and partly as a result of the relatively poor quality of their interactions with other people (Porter *et al.* 1997). There remains an enduring difficulty in enabling the entitlement of pupils with SLD/PMLD to access a National Curriculum, which demands that all pupils should be able to express themselves clearly in both speech and writing, use grammatically correct sentences, spell, punctuate and otherwise communicate effectively (SCAA 1997a).

One would expect pupils to develop effective oral and written communication skills as an outcome of their participation within English lessons, even though the teaching of English, in a general sense, is considered to be problematical because of the irregular nature of the English language (White 1995). Yet the task of making English accessible and meaningful to pupils with SLD/PMLD is so much greater than just having to cope with the irregularities of the language itself (Locke 1994). There is no guarantee that pupils with SLD/PMLD can be appropriately engaged within the teaching of English, or that they will ever be able to communicate effectively as an outcome of their participation within English lessons (Aird 2000b). Difficulties that are encountered when teaching English to pupils with SLD/PMLD will inevitably inhibit the ability of these pupils to become effective learners.

In recent times, the QCA has recommended that the teaching of literacy, a functional communication skill, should be taught during specific lessons. The QCA invested heavily during the late 1990s in demonstrating how literacy can best be taught via so-called 'Literacy Hours' that are organised in addition to, and outside, traditional English lessons. Although some attention was directed as to how the Literacy Hour might be organised in SLD schools (Bainbridge 1999), little attention was paid to the fact that pupils with SLD/PMLD do not develop functional communication skills according to any generalised pattern of development and, as a consequence, might require a different teaching strategy.

Moreover, pupils with SLD/PMLD do not only have difficulties in developing effective communication skills (Nind and Hewitt 1998); they also have difficulties in acquiring language and using language appropriately (Goldbart 1986). In an SLD school, functional communication skills should not be taught independently from the overarching English curriculum. The acquisition of language, the use of language and the development of functional communication skills are intrinsically linked, and the English curriculum is the means by which a school should ensure consistency in teaching these skills.

Engaging pupils with SLD/PMLD in a broad curriculum makes it difficult to exercise control over the breadth of new language to which pupils are likely to be exposed. Subjects within the entitlement curriculum, such as Mathematics, rely upon the abilities of pupils to acquire the language of mathematics in order for them to develop their understanding about mathematical concepts (DfEE 1999b). Pupils in an average SLD school are likely to participate in all subjects of the National Curriculum, in environments that may be rich in new language but where they are probably unable to acquire and use that new language in any functional or meaningful sense. The language of tuition, used for the teaching of the whole curriculum, should not extend beyond a pupil's ability to acquire and/or use new language appropriately. SLD schools need to exercise control over the use of language and communication, across the whole curriculum, and ensure that teaching methodologies operate within meaningful terms of reference.

It has been said that engaging pupils with SLD/PMLD in subjects of the National Curriculum provides these pupils with interesting contexts in which learning can take place (Byers 1999). However, considerable care needs to be taken to ensure that the pupils being taught are able to make sense of these interesting contexts. Pupils with PMLD, in particular, are unlikely to recognise the significance of the majority of learning experiences in which they find themselves involved (Bradley 1998). For some profoundly disabled pupils, it is unlikely that they will *ever* be able to progress from using the most basic levels of interaction. At the most basic level, these interactions are in the form of involuntary reflex actions, carried out to maintain a sense of security (Brown *et al.* 1998). These ways of interacting have been described as a child's primitive reflexive and reactive responses to the outside world (Coupe-O'Kane and Goldbart 1998) and are far removed from the more sophisticated stages of language acquisition and functional use of language. For pupils who rely on these very basic levels of interaction, it is essential that every effort is made to control the teaching environment so that a pupil's reflexive and/or reactive actions are recognised and consistently reinforced.

Every learning experience, regardless of how interesting the context might be, needs to be presented at a level that will encourage pupils with SLD/PMLD to develop functional communication skills and progress beyond a stage of merely reacting to their environment in an involuntary way. Following the need to maintain emotional security and basic comfort, the need to communicate meaningfully should be considered as an absolute priority when teaching profoundly disabled pupils (Nind and Hewitt 1998). Some pupils with SLD/PMLD rely on the use of elementary reflexes, such as gaze, to have any sort of meaningful dialogue with others (Field 1977), and this level of functional communication, which is the key to learning across the whole curriculum, will remain at that pre-verbal and pre-symbolic level. Classroom environments and learning contexts that are organised to make learning interesting need to be empathetic to pupils who communicate at this level.

Pupils with SLD/PMLD are unlikely to benefit from teaching that relies solely upon oral and written communications, or from teaching in which the language of tuition is too complex. The use of augmentative communication systems, such as sign-assisted speech and the use of symbols, to represent vocabulary, may help some pupils to communicate. However, the level at which the language is pitched will determine whether or not an individual pupil will ever benefit from such augmentative and symbolic techniques. Teachers need to beware, therefore, of importing mainstream initiatives that use symbolic representation, such as the Literacy Hour, with the naïve expectation that pupils with SLD/PMLD will learn functional communication skills, according to any sort of generalised pattern of development.

The organisation of the English curriculum in SLD schools should be very different from its organisation in other types of school. The English curriculum in the SLD school needs to reflect the language and communication difficulties that are innate in pupils with SLD/PMLD. The English curriculum should include curriculum material that relates to:

- aspects of language acquisition that have traditionally featured as part of the developmental curriculum commonly utilised in schools for pupils with SLD/PMLD and taught via a total communication methodology to ensure that the language of tuition is tightly controlled;
- the use of functional communication skills across the whole curriculum, including the use of intensive interaction techniques, use of language, augmentative communication, reading and writing;
- material from National Curriculum English, such as the use of poetry, drama etc., that can be used to enrich a pupil's use of language and provide motivating contexts to practise new language;
- speech- and language-therapy treatments in response to speech and language disabilities.

In order for an English curriculum to be effective, it is important that the subject has clear terms of reference. The following statements (adapted from SCAA 1997a) are believed to provide a useful starting point for agreeing such terms of reference:

- The content of an English curriculum should provide unambiguous information about the knowledge, understanding and skills that pupils are expected to develop in pre-verbal communication, language acquisition, functional use of language, and oral and written communications.
- The organisation of an English curriculum should reflect what is known about patterns of language development in disabled pupils.
- Teaching and organisational strategies should take account of the personal learning styles of pupils, and this information should be used to ensure appropriate differentiation and engagement of pupils in the teaching of language and communication across the whole curriculum.
- Teaching and organisational strategies should give high status to securing a consistent learning environment with which to promote functional communication skills.

- There should be clear systems for monitoring and evaluating pupil progression within English across the whole curriculum.
- The design of the English curriculum should supply a consistent teaching methodology and a consistent and purposeful use of resources.

As has already been established, the use of language throughout the whole curriculum needs to be carefully controlled. The content of the English curriculum should extend from the teaching of basic communication skills to that of incorporating clearly defined core and extension vocabularies with which to supply the language of tuition across the whole curriculum. A core vocabulary is required to aid basic language acquisition and to provide pupils with sufficient language with which to promote cognition and understanding. This careful control of language is essential for helping pupils to develop an elementary understanding of the world around them and to begin to influence things in an intentional way, thus reinforcing their desire to use language as a means of communicating (Kersner and Wright 1996). This is particularly so for pupils who rely on assisted and/or augmentative communication systems, where their potential to develop functional communication skills might be restricted by the limitations of their preferred augmentative system (Graves 2000).

The content of a core vocabulary needs to be sufficiently flexible so as to reflect the chronological age of pupils and the types of life experiences that they are likely to participate in. It has been argued that a core vocabulary needs to reflect the pyramid of human need (Graves 2000), corresponding to expressions of need (Newman and Beail, 1994, adapted) within a child's:

- emotions;
- behaviours;
- functions;
- physiology;
- self-determination.

The content of a core vocabulary ought therefore to include the names of objects, people, places and actions that a pupil needs to acquire in order to make sense of the world and influence events. In addition to the acquisition of nouns and verbs, pupils will also need vocabulary to help them develop a basic grammatical competence with which to express themselves. In order for a pupil to develop a sense of self-determination, a vocabulary of prepositions, adjectives and conjunctions will also be necessary, in order that he or she may be able to express preferences and dislikes. The size of such a core vocabulary is a matter of conjecture; what is important is that a school enables its pupils to acquire and use language in a pragmatic way, so that the desire and ability to communicate is empowered.

The teaching of a core vocabulary needs to be undertaken via a whole-school, total-communication strategy, so that pupils who use alternatives to speech have the same opportunity to benefit from a common functional vocabulary. The content of a core vocabulary also needs to be multimodal and incorporate signs, symbols and objects of reference (Detheridge and Detheridge 1997). It should be remembered that, when the acquisition of words from a core vocabulary is being taught, the language and communication abilities of many pupils will not follow generalised patterns of development (Locke 1999). As a consequence, pragmatic approaches will be required to allow some 'hard to reach' pupils the opportunity to acquire language from the environment in a practical, cause-and-effect way, and also to assist a pupil's idiosyncratic way of interacting to bring about predictable changes in the immediate environment (Nind and Hewett 1998).

Vocabulary that extends beyond the school's core vocabulary should be introduced and taught in a purposeful, structured manner. For example, if pupils are expected to participate in Mathematics lessons and learn about numbers, calculations, shape, space and measures, they must be taught the appropriate vocabulary. The extent of this additional vocabulary will need to be determined by the concepts that teachers wish pupils to learn as a consequence of their teaching (Coupe-O'Kane and Goldbart 1998). How individual pupils might progress within such vocabulary will depend upon their personal ability to acquire and use language appropriately. Close collaboration between teachers is essential in order that subject-specific vocabularies can be agreed on a whole-school basis and differentiation of those vocabularies undertaken according to the abilities of individual pupils.

An SLD school must decide on what needs to be included within the English curriculum in order to promote effective language acquisition, use of language, and functional communication skills. Having agreed *what* should be included in the English curriculum, a school will need to decide *how* that curriculum can best be delivered. Schools need to be pragmatic and honest in the way they go about this. There is insufficient time available in a typical SLD school day to devote one hour purely to the teaching of literacy; however, it is essential that at least one hour a day is dedicated to the teaching of English in a holistic way. It is worth remembering that the teaching of English to pupils with SLD/PMLD should be fun. This is not just because a fun element within teaching is a good way of motivating pupils to learn more readily, but out of recognition of the fact that a good many pupils with SLD/PMLD find communication particularly frustrating. The last thing staff should want to do is to compound that frustration by making the learning of English boring and sterile.

Teaching activities that have a high dramatic content are known to be effective in actively engaging pupils with SLD/PMLD in the learning process, as well as providing opportunities to introduce a fun element into teaching. Drama has been shown to be an excellent medium for helping pupils develop the narrative mode of thought (Bruner 1975) that is so important for promoting their active engagement in stories, poetry, reading and writing and for obtaining the maximum benefit from these conventional ways of teaching English (Hinchcliffe 1996). The use of drama has also been found to be very helpful in teaching pupils with ASD about empathy and emotions (Peter 2000) and to help them make progress within the triad of impairment (Wing 1996). Drama appeals to the innate sense of playfulness, thus providing an excellent medium in which to teach functional language in settings that are motivating and as realistic as we wish to make them (Peter 2000).

The use of interactive stories is a good example of how language and communication can be taught using teaching strategies with a dramatic element. For pupils with a profound disability, who are functioning at reflexive and reactive pre-verbal stages of communication, interactive social stories can be used to incorporate sound, textures and rhythms in a multi-modal way to help pupils access the English curriculum (Fuller 1999). The use of sound, in particular, has been found to be very helpful in capturing the attention of pupils with SLD/PMLD (Brudenell 1987).

The teaching of literacy in the SLD school needs to be different from that recommended for non-disabled, mainstream pupils. Literacy activities need to be suitable for pupils who will not progress beyond pre-reading competencies, as well as for those who will be able to develop functional levels of reading competency. Teachers in SLD schools need to remember that it is unlikely that the literacy skills of their pupils will follow any normal pattern of development. Literacy materials therefore need to allow for extensive lateral learning so that pupils may use their basic abilities in a functional sense across the whole curriculum. There is little value in 'pushing' a pupil through a commercial reading scheme, in which they might be able to recognise and name the shape of words, if at the end of it they have little real understanding of the language that has been used or the events that have been depicted. Literacy materials should have a strong bias towards real life, especially for older pupils who need to develop the ability to apply their functional reading and writing skills in practical ways to aid their social inclusion.

The additional disabilities that affect many pupils with SLD/PMLD need to be considered when these pupils are taught *how* to read. The re-emergence of the importance of phonics, for the teaching of literacy to mainstream pupils, does not have the same relevance in the SLD school. Pupils with SLD/PMLD typically have inadequate phonological awareness and/or innate auditory memory problems, which make it unlikely that they will ever be able to develop functional phonological abilities (Aird 2000b). Findings from research undertaken in Lewisham and North Southwark Health Authority (1984–1991) indicated that approximately 80 per cent of people with learning disabilities have impaired hearing. This high incidence of hearing impairment also needs to be considered when literacy skills are taught to pupils with SLD/PMLD. Inadequate phonological awareness, poor auditory memory and a high incidence of hearing impairment in pupils with SLD/PMLD all argue against the use of a phonetic approach when teaching literacy skills. The use of sight recognition is advocated as being the preferred and principal means of teaching literacy to pupils with SLD/PMLD (Aird 2000b).

The teaching of Mathematics

The Mathematics curriculum is generally considered to be linear because of the way in which mathematical skills have to be learned according to a preordained order. This linear characteristic might suggest that Mathematics is a subject that pupils with SLD/PMLD would immediately find problematical because of the difficulties these pupils have in developing their skills in a linear fashion. It is probably for this reason that Mathematics has not always featured as a subject in its own right in the traditional SLD curriculum. Numeracy has tended to represent Mathematics in the SLD curriculum because of its value as a functional life skill. The broader applications and attributes of Mathematics have not enjoyed the same high profile and the introduction of the Numeracy Hour, as part of the National Framework for Mathematics (DfEE 1999b), is likely to reinforce this traditional view (Robbins 2000).

Mathematics, in the SLD school, needs to have a much broader teaching base than the provision of a dedicated Numeracy Hour if pupils are to develop meaningful concepts about the principles that govern their environment. Mathematics is a subject that can enable pupils with SLD/PMLD to perceive similarities and differences in their environment and begin to formulate concepts to help them order that environment (Porter 2000). The ability to assimilate information from the environment, understand the meaning of what has been assimilated and develop meaningful concepts about the principles that govern the environment are all invaluable for preparing pupils for the adult world. Mathematics is the basis upon which problem-solving and decision-making skills are founded (Banes

1999), and the subject has the luxury of allowing information to be assimilated in a concrete way (Longhorn 2000).

It is worrying that no SLD schools were included in the national pilot of the National Framework for Mathematics, and this omission makes it more likely that the framework will not be immediately relevant to the learning styles typical of pupils with SLD/PMLD. For example, a reliance upon oral methods for the teaching of numeracy, such as in the framework's reliance upon mental arithmetic, is not in empathy with what we know about how pupils with SLD/PMLD learn. Pupils with SLD/PMLD typically have relatively poor auditory memory, when compared with their mainstream peers, and tend to rely heavily upon visual modes of learning. Although early trials of mental arithmetic exercises showed some increase in the ability of pupils with SLD/PMLD to make progress within these exercises (Harris and Thompson 2000), research shows that such an emphasis actually results in lowered standards of numeracy, as compared with mathematics teaching that has a much broader base (Teacher Training Agency 1999).

It makes sense to allocate valuable curriculum time to the teaching of Mathematics, a subject that is important for helping to prepare pupils with SLD/PMLD to cope with the demands of modern living (Robbins 2000). However, simply seeking to promote the arithmetical abilities of pupils is not sufficient reason for commandeering valuable teaching time. The teaching of Mathematics in the SLD school requires a framework that is altogether different from that employed in the mainstream. Such a framework will need to use a variety of real-life contexts to stimulate assimilation and use of information, provide pupils with opportunities for meaningful problem-solving experiences, and enable those pupils to formulate concepts about the principles that govern their immediate environment.

The teaching of ICT

Regardless of any specific benefits that might accrue to pupils in SLD schools as a consequence of teaching them ICT, the fact that society continues to be so dramatically affected by the rapid advances in information and communications technology would demand in itself that ICT has a recognised place in the core curriculum. Pupils with SLD/PMLD – in the same manner that applies for all other schoolchildren – need to be prepared to participate in lifestyles that are increasingly being influenced by ICT.

ICT has the potential to promote independent living and self-determination by the use of switch technology. Once an understanding of cause and effect has been established, a profoundly disabled pupil can use switch technology to provide an augmentative means of communicating and to control aspects of their immediate environment. A pupil's mobility may be enhanced and ICT used to access the environment and gather information in ways that would otherwise be denied.

Through good teaching, ICT can lead to relatively sophisticated levels of self-supported learning, empowering pupils to be able to gather and analyse information in ways that could never have been dreamed of in the past. When used on a small-group basis, ICT can also promote teamworking skills, with opportunities for pupils with varying physical abilities to produce work of a relatively high standard of presentation.

A particular benefit of ICT is its multimodal capability, with opportunities to combine sound, pictures, symbols and graphics and be responsive to an individual pupil's preferences and abilities. There are endless permutations available for the promotion of functional cross-curricular skills such as communication, literacy, problem solving and decision making. Some of the 'hard-to-teach' concepts from subjects of the peripheral curriculum can also be made more accessible by the use of CD-ROMs.

However, the benefit of teaching ICT to pupils with SLD/PMLD can only be as good as the facilities a school has available and the ability and willingness of staff to ensure that pupils access ICT in a purposeful way. ICT needs to be well resourced and well organised, and good ICT practice needs to be thoroughly disseminated to all staff, if it is to be of any value.

It is worth remembering that there are also limitations in what ICT can actually achieve on behalf of pupils with SLD/PMLD. Impressive technology must not be allowed to disguise shortcomings in the provision of low-technology teaching aids. For instance, ICT cannot augment communication on behalf of a profoundly disabled pupil if that pupil has never been taught the rudiments of communicating. There are aspects of communication that are best augmented with low-technology aids that are reliable, transferable, and designed specifically with a particular pupil's needs in mind. It would be ethically wrong for a school to provide pupils with the technology to communicate and control their immediate environment if that same provision could not be guaranteed for the pupils' life outside school. Low-technology aids are more likely to be continued after a pupil has left school, and pupils must not be made reliant upon expensive, high-technology aids if these cannot continue once schooling is finished.

The management of ICT is a complex task. Schools need to be clear about the skills they want pupils to learn as a consequence of engaging them in ICT lessons, and the use of ICT must not be allowed to become an end in itself. ICT has particularly good potential for cross-curricular application, and schools need to have a clear map of how it is to be used to support learning across the whole curriculum. The selection and management of software needs careful consideration if it is not to become confused and divorced from the ICT curriculum itself. Finally, there is the onerous task of managing the hardware. Increasing standards of technical knowledge are becoming necessary, as the range and complexity of ICT equipment continues to expand. Schools need to consider carefully how the hardware that supports the ICT curriculum is to be maintained. Pupils with SLD/PMLD are unlikely to tolerate access to ICT if the quality of their experience is not satisfactory.

Setting targets within the core curriculum

Although there has been advice about *what* teachers in SLD schools should be teaching with regard to the National Curriculum, it is not always easy for a class teacher in a typical SLD school to know exactly *what* their pupils need to learn as a matter of priority from their time in the classroom. It is also not easy for these teachers to know *how* to teach their pupils. There is no one strategy for teaching pupils with SLD/PMLD that is capable of meeting all of their needs (Smith 1991). Indeed, a combination of strategies is required to link together IEP targets and targets relating to subjects of the National Curriculum, so that learning priorities can be addressed via lesson plans that are coherent and purposeful (McNicholas 2000). Such a combination needs to be able to inform teachers of *what* they should be teaching, *how* they should be teaching it and also, importantly, to *whom* (Brown *et al.* 1998).

There is much that a school can do to facilitate effective teaching and learning across the whole curriculum. Having a clearly defined idea of what a school wishes its pupils to learn, as a matter of priority, is a useful and logical starting point. When considering the priorities of pupils with SLD/PMLD, IEP targets should head the list of priorities that a school agrees upon. IEP targets should have direct links with the circumstances of a pupil's disability, intrinsically associated with the maintenance of their well-being and should be additional to, or different from, a pupil's needs within the organisation of the National Curriculum (DfEE 2000b).

Once a school has identified a pupil's personal learning style and agreed his or her priority needs, as determined against the assessment criteria relating to the specialist curriculum, the selection of IEP targets should be straightforward and their content unambiguous. Ensuring that a pupil's IEP targets are properly addressed within the organisation of a school day should also be a fairly straightforward task, and some advice on systems for managing IEP targets is provided in Chapter 7. Subjects of the specialist curriculum obviously need to be clearly defined and organised in a manner whereby the curriculum material can be applied consistently and coherently across a school. Having a clearly defined specialist curriculum also enables a school to organise teaching resources and special facilities so as to minimise the handicapping effects of disability and to ensure that the learning potential of individual pupils is not unduly restricted because of the implications of a particular impairment.

Addressing the IEP targets of individual pupils requires dedicated, quality time in order for staff to respond to the educational, caring and treatment implications of disability. This time may be directed toward teaching pertinent skills from a clearly defined specialist curriculum and/or toward implementing treatment and therapy regimes as prescribed by therapists and medical staff. Some IEP targets, relating to this latter category, may need to be addressed in relative isolation from the rest of the curriculum because of their insular and/or intimate nature. However, some IEP targets will need to be applied across the whole curriculum and incorporated into the daily dynamics of teaching and learning (SCAA 1996b). In order for them to be effective, IEP targets need to be based upon a sound, coherent, specialist curriculum, as agreed by a team of professionals working in collaboration (Marvin 1998). A pupil's progress within his or her IEP targets will need to be measured partly by anecdotal evidence relating to subtle changes in personal learning style, and partly by empirical evidence relating to performance during teaching activities drawn from the specialist curriculum.

All of the conventional subjects at the core of the SLD curriculum (i.e. English and Communication, Mathematics and ICT) have skills that need to be applied across the whole curriculum in order for pupils to be able to learn effectively. These skills need to be taught during subject-specific lessons before they can be generalised and applied effectively across the whole curriculum. Because the skills associated with these three subjects are often prerequisites for enabling effective learning to take place in a general sense, it is right to consider them as priorities within the education of pupils with SLD/PMLD. The setting of curriculum targets for individual pupils needs to be based upon these three core subjects, particularly upon developing skills that operate across the whole curriculum.

If the curriculum content pertaining to the three core subjects is sufficiently detailed and robust, it is a relatively easy task to establish curriculum targets on behalf of individual pupils that will make sense to both pupil and teacher. Curriculum targets need to be achievable and measurable from a clear baseline. They also need to be worthwhile for the pupil and suitably challenging (Rose *et al.* 1999). Curriculum targets can be incremental and linear, to an extent, but they also need to allow for considerable lateral learning and award proper status to the generalisation of emerging skills. Disabled pupils are notoriously difficult to teach (Ware 1996), and therefore it is important that the targets chosen to represent priorities within their education are ones that provide a functional purpose and make pupils' learning more effective. For instance, communication skills need to be applied laterally, in a variety of contexts, if they are to be useful to a pupil and enable them to benefit meaningfully from access to a broad and balanced curriculum. Likewise, problem-solving skills, which have their home in Mathematics, need to be applied laterally if they are to be useful in a functional sense and help enable a pupil to become an effective learner.

Teaching the subjects of the peripheral curriculum

There is a requirement upon all schools to deliver a broad and balanced curriculum, such as that represented by the National Curriculum. Although the actual breadth and balance of the National Curriculum may have varied over time as a consequence of revisions undertaken by successive governments, there has remained a fairly consistent notion of what teachers are required to teach pupils at the four Key Stages. To assist with the task of teaching subjects of the National Curriculum to pupils with SLD/PMLD, flexibility for teaching toward Statements of Attainment (SoAs), from each of the Key Stages, was introduced in recognition that some pupils might require longer than two years to attain the SoA relevant to their chronological age (see, for example, Dearing 1994 and NCC 1992).

There should be little room for debate, therefore, about what teachers should be aiming to teach pupils with SLD/PMLD about subjects of the National Curriculum. The National Curriculum provides a framework of SoAs that teachers can address in a flexible way so that the content of their teaching can reflect the ability levels of their pupils. In response to curriculum overload, which is a perennial problem in all types of school, there is also flexibility to allow schools to organise pupil access to different subjects on a cyclical programme, so that the full breadth of the National Curriculum may be addressed at some time during a pupil's school career and thus compensate for the manner in which other learning priorities might make an impact upon access to the full National Curriculum. After placing English and Communication, Mathematics and ICT at the core of the SLD curriculum, the remaining subjects of the National Curriculum may be considered as representing an SLD school's peripheral curriculum (see Figure 6.3).

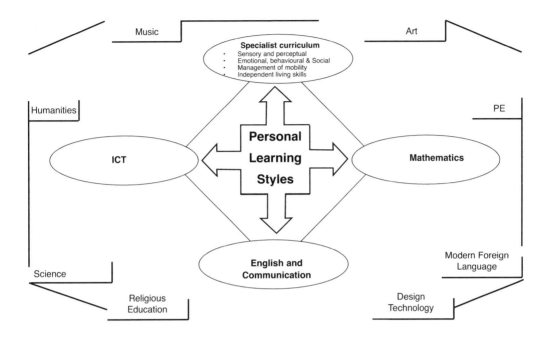

Figure 6:3 Subjects of the peripheral curriculum placed within the whole curriculum

All lessons in the SLD school, regardless of the subject being taught, need to include a similar basic structure if they are to be successful in engaging pupils appropriately. Figure 6.4 illustrates what needs to be considered when planning a common lesson-plan structure.

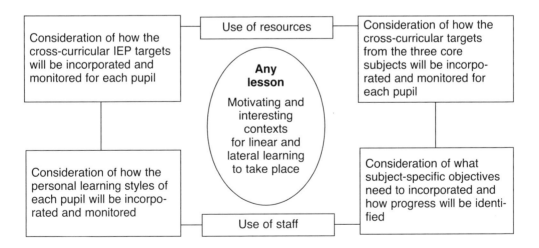

Figure 6.4 A common lesson-plan structure for the peripheral curriculum

In order to implement a common lesson-plan structure, it is first necessary for a school to have in place a clearly defined peripheral curriculum that is sufficiently prescriptive so as to avoid duplication and/or omission of curriculum material for individual classes and/or year groups. A school needs to have a clearly defined map that indicates *what* teachers are expected to teach, together with Key Stage plans that indicate *when* it is to be taught. It is the responsibility of a school's SMT to put such a map in place, in consultation and negotiation with subject coordinators. Individual teachers cannot be expected to determine either curriculum balance and/or the pacing of new curriculum material in isolation. However, with appropriate support and the benefit of clear curriculum mapping, teachers can be expected to produce lesson plans that are realistic, relevant and meaningful.

P levels have the potential to provide a very useful guide for teachers to plan *how* to teach subjects from the peripheral curriculum so that they provide meaningful, as well as interesting, contexts for learning. However, this advice is offered with the strong caveat that P levels are not appropriate for assessing and reporting the progress of pupils with SLD/PMLD within *all* the subjects of the National Curriculum. P levels can help teachers to differentiate the content of the National Curriculum; however, teachers must not regard the content of P levels as being properly representative of the specialist curriculum that the majority of pupils with SLD/PMLD require in order to respond to the educational and caring implications of their individual disabilities. At best, P levels are a useful tool for differentiating the early levels of the peripheral curriculum.

The personal learning styles of pupils need to be given priority status within the organisation and delivery of the peripheral curriculum, because personal learning styles provide the setting conditions for enabling pupils to participate in lessons and make it more likely for them to learn. On occasion, the need to get setting conditions right must have absolute priority within the organisation of everyday teaching. Staff need to be guided by observation of the subtle changes in each pupil's personal learning style and be sufficiently flexible to adapt lesson plans in response to the needs of pupils. Particularly when working with pupils with PMLD, staff need to seize moments when a pupil is actively seeking to interact with peers, adults or events (Ware 1996), and maintain the setting conditions that have triggered such moments, in order to enable these pupils to demonstrate lateral progress within their personal learning style. If we ignore the way a pupil is responding during a lesson and instead only direct attention towards the things we wish to teach, then there is a risk that some pupils – particularly those with more profound disabilities and those with severe challenging behaviour – will be subjected to what have been described as 'secondary motivational handicaps'

(Seligman 1975). In other words, if the personal learning styles of pupils are not granted sufficient status within the management of a lesson, some pupils are likely to challenge the staff by either opting out or by resorting to disruptive behaviour.

Evidence that pupils with SLD/PMLD are suitably engaged in a lesson may not be demonstrable from simple analysis of their performance against a linear sequence of predetermined learning objectives. Such evidence may only come from the monitoring of a pupil's personal learning style within the dynamics of everyday lessons. For instance, if a pupil's rate of self-injurious behaviour is consistently less during certain lessons and/or activities within a lesson, this may be evidence that the pupil is appropriately engaged and is making progress. Such progress is not based upon any hierarchical linear sequence but is demonstrable by the manner in which a pupil responds to the setting conditions within a classroom. It is worth remembering that the peripheral curriculum is intended to enrich the context in which learning takes place. When pupils with SLD/PMLD are enabled to access a broad curriculum, they are provided with opportunities to generalise skills that are essential for functional living, in learning contexts that are interesting and that will help them experience the richness of life. Engagement in a broad and balanced curriculum helps nurture the development of the whole child.

The assessment of pupil progress within the peripheral curriculum

In the drive to keep the flame of entitlement alive, the use of P levels has featured as the most prominent strategy used in recent times. The National Curriculum is based upon the notion that the quality of learning is only demonstrable when pupils can be seen to attain specific linear attainment levels. The P level initiative was created in that likeness, despite what was known about the tendency of pupils with SLD/PMLD to be unable to acquire skills and knowledge according to any predetermined linear sequence. The development of P levels was also undertaken despite what was known about the folly of seeking to over-formularise early-years curricula in this way (Owens 1997).

There was an obvious rationale for P levels to be considered for use in this linear way. Traditions of small-stepping and task analysis (Porter 1986) are sufficiently well ingrained in SLD practice to suggest that small-stepping learning objectives relating to Level 1 for the subjects in the National Curriculum, will provide teachers with knowledge of how to teach National Curriculum subjects. There is no doubt that task analysis is a very useful teaching technique that, at times, makes learning possible for some pupils with SLD/PMLD. However, it is wrong to assume that this strategy can be combined with elements of the traditional SLD development curriculum so that the assessment of pupil performance within the SLD school can function in the same way as assessment in a mainstream school.

The use of linear sequencing in the subjects of the National Curriculum makes it very difficult to teach the National Curriculum to pupils who consistently fail to make measurable progress on notional patterns of child development (Ware and Healey 1994). This is not to say that the educational content of subjects of the National Curriculum is irrelevant to the needs of these pupils. The subjects of the National Curriculum have been shown to provide interesting contexts for learning to take place (Byers 1999). However, recognising that these subjects can provide interesting contexts for learning to take place is not the same as suggesting that the education of pupils with SLD/PMLD should be reconceptualised according to the principles that underpin mainstream education (Sebba and Rose 1992). Before the introduction of the National Curriculum, it was known that moves towards literate modes of learning in western Europe, as typified by the National Curriculum, were inappropriate for the learning styles characteristic of pupils with SEN (Gardner 1984). Because it is often difficult to define clear learning outcomes for pupils with SEN, the quality of the curriculum that is used to teach these pupils is often perceived as being less important than the linear and literate National Curriculum wherein the quality of learning can be endorsed by empirical evidence (Sebba *et al.* 1995).

The use of National Curriculum P levels as a method for assessing and publicising the abilities of pupils with SLD/PMLD is particularly worrying, because it seeks to reconceptualise SLD practice according to mainstream principles. Clear advice has been published to caution against the use of P levels as a linear assessment framework for pupils with SLD/PMLD (University of Durham 1999) and yet the trend continues. The sensory-perceptual teaching approaches that have been imported into the P level framework are not precise teaching techniques. The anticipated outcomes of sensory-perceptual teaching – i.e. the skills and knowledge that pupils are expected to learn as a consequence of the teaching – cannot be stated in the same empirical and objective terms as those that SoAs are able to do for the ordinary levels of the National Curriculum. This is because the responses of pupils who operate at a sensory-perceptual level are limited to very subtle changes in behaviour that might, or might not, be retained and/or generalised. Hence, the only types of evidence that can be used to demonstrate a pupil's behaviour during the teaching of a subject's basic P levels is that of anecdotal evidence. This evidence is not the same as the empirical evidence that is used to demonstrate evidence of attainment in levels of the National Curriculum and should not be regarded as such.

Teaching pupils with SLD/PMLD often requires different assessment strategies to demonstrate the effectiveness of teaching to those conventional strategies employed in mainstream schools (Barber and Goldbart 1998). Monitoring the effectiveness of teaching subjects within the peripheral curriculum to pupils with PMLD, in particular, can often only be done by gathering anecdotal evidence about subtle changes of behaviour in response to different teaching strategies. This evidence tends to be anecdotal because the changes are too subtle to be organised into any sort of generalised linear pattern of development and because they tend to be of a very idiosyncratic nature, recognisable only to the one or two members of staff who know a particular pupil very well.

Various authors have suggested that these subtle behavioural changes by pupils can be classified into a common pattern (McInnes and Treffrey 1982; Aitken and Buultjens 1992; Brown 1996). Brown (1996) classified these behaviours according to a pattern of seven levels, representing different stages in a pupil's developing internal-learning process:

- encounter;
- awareness;
- response;
- engagement;
- participation;
- involvement;
- attainment.

Without very clear and unambiguous assessment criteria, the progress of a pupil along the first four levels of this scale can only be judged by anecdotal evidence, which is likely to be recognisable only to staff who work most closely with the pupil. There is no single behaviour, common to all pupils, that can be used to indicate when profoundly disabled pupils progress from the level of encounter, for example, to that of awareness. The behaviours of profoundly disabled pupils are constrained – and partly dictated – by the extent of their various disabilities. These behaviours are idiosyncratic to an individual pupil in much the same way as their individual disabilities are.

However, it may be possible to interpret an individual pupil's subtle behaviours according to how successfully they are participating during an activity. Whether or not these changes in behaviour denote that learning has actually taken place is

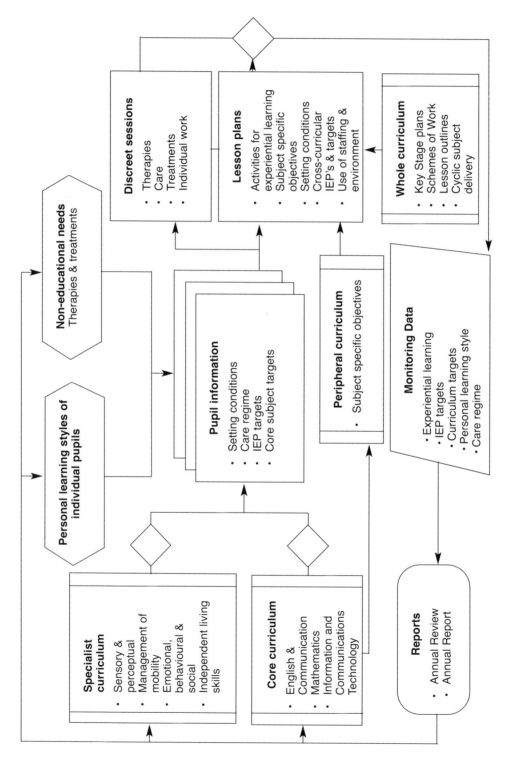

Figure 6.5 A process for managing the whole curriculum

another matter entirely. It is more likely that these changes of behaviour indicate whether the setting conditions provided during a particular lesson are appropriate to an individual pupil's personal learning style and/or whether the pupil is feeling secure and physically well at that particular time. There are many variables in the lives of profoundly disabled pupils to consider when monitoring these kinds of behavioural changes; not all of these variables will be in the control of the teacher or relevant to the topic that is being taught. Empirical evidence of the progress of profoundly disabled pupils can only be realistically sought by monitoring their performance within the more clinically based specialist curriculum, and within therapeutic and treatment regimes.

A process for managing delivery of the whole curriculum

It is unrealistic to expect teachers to plan, deliver and monitor the education of the pupils in their class without reference to a school process for managing the whole curriculum. Every school is different and, as such, there cannot be a definitive guide of how to go about developing processes for managing the curriculum; each school needs to develop its own. However, an example of a suggested process for managing the whole curriculum has been provided in Figure 6.5, and a school SMT might find this illustration a useful prompt for discussing how the individual needs of pupils can be linked into the organisation of the whole curriculum.

CHAPTER 7

Management of the learning environment

The pressures of working with pupils with SLD/PMLD

Pupils with SLD/PMLD typically have disabilities that are in addition to their underlying difficulties, requiring the support of a wide range of specialist services. Many of these pupils also have serious medical conditions and require nursing and the provision of medical treatments. A good number of them also require individually designed packages of care, in order to maintain their well-being, comfort and security. This diverse range of needs means that it is impossible for any one service provider, or practitioner, ever to hope of meeting all of the needs of pupils with SLD/PMLD (Lacey 1998). As a consequence, SLD schools are typically multi-agency by function. They are required to coordinate the provision of specialist services from an LEA, local health authority, social services department and a variety of voluntary organisations, in addition to fulfilling their basic role of providing a relevant education for their pupils. The multi-agency function of SLD schools, however, has received relatively little attention compared with their role as child educators.

The role of teachers is fairly generic across all phases and sectors of education. This generic role is one that is reinforced by national conditions of employment and a common framework for appraising teacher performance. The performance of teachers, in particular, has been subject to increasing attention and has featured heavily both in the OFSTED framework of school inspection and in recent guidelines on the performance management of teachers (DfEE 2000a). This generic interpretation of the role of teachers has helped to establish a culture of teacher domination in SLD schools (Sebba *et al.* 1995), despite the multi-agency function of these schools.

The culture of teacher domination in SLD schools is likely to be reinforced by the introduction of initiatives such as the Literacy Hour and Numeracy Hour. Recent educational reform has been increasingly prescriptive, not just about *what* teachers should teach but also about *how* teachers should teach. The prescriptive nature of this reform has sought to stereotype teaching methods in an effort to make teaching more effective. The recommended methods prescribed for teaching the Literacy and Numeracy Hours, for example, were developed with the intention of raising standards in levels of pupil literacy and numeracy. Thus, society has developed clear views about the role of the teacher and about how teachers should conduct their business, regardless of the type of school in which they provide their services.

Guidelines for managing the performance of teachers and the promotion of stereotyped teaching methods were introduced long after initial specialist teacher-training in the education of pupils with SLD/PMLD ceased to be maintained. Since the demise of this specialist training in the mid-1980s, SLD schools have had a diminishing pool of specially trained teachers from which to recruit, and this has resulted in diminishing standards of knowledge about the aetiology and pedagogy of disability being available to these schools. Evidence from 72 LEAs, surveyed in the year 2000, showed that one-third of teachers in SLD schools had no SEN qualification; and this lack of specialist training was reported by the teachers themselves to be adversely affecting their ability to understand the needs of their pupils and be able to make appropriate provision for them (McNicholas 2000). SLD schools have not had sufficient specialist knowledge to enable them to challenge the imposition of educational reform and advocate the need for educational strategies that are specific to the needs of pupils with SLD/PMLD. Hence, SLD school practice has tended to fall into line with mainstream school practice, with the very unfortunate consequence that increasing numbers of pupils with challenging needs have had to be accommodated in privately funded specialist residential schools (Christ Church College 1996).

The handicapping characteristics of disability are generally caused by society's failure to understand the implications of disability and make proper provision for individuals who are disabled (Oliver 1996). Given the number of specialists who work in SLD schools and who are expert in various aspects of disability, it ought to be the case that SLD schools function as models of good practice in making proper provision for disabled pupils. However, the evidence to support such a role model does not always appear to be born out in practice. A survey of provision for MSI pupils, conducted jointly by the DfEE and SENSE, revealed that specialist curricular provision for pupils with this disability was not readily demonstrable in SLD schools, despite the fact that some staff in these schools appeared to be aware of the need for such specialist provision (Porter *et al.* 1997). This is further evidence that a difficulty in teachers being able to properly understand, and make provision for, the special needs of their pupils creates weaknesses in the ability of a school as a whole to respond to the demands of pupils with SLD/PMLD, regardless of what specialist multi-agency support might be available.

The fact that external pressures have been allowed to erode the development of good practice in provision for pupils with SLD/PMLD is regrettable. This is especially so, given the problems that are inherent in teaching these pupils. There are significant emotional pressures that impact upon teachers working in these schools that are peculiar to working with disabled pupils. Unless these pressures are appropriately addressed, teachers in SLD schools may well experience further constraint in their ability to respond appropriately to the needs of their pupils.

The limited interpersonal abilities of individuals with PMLD, for example, have been found to make working in the PMLD sector particularly difficult and less satisfying than that experienced in other working environments (Ware 1996). The lack of feedback that teachers can experience when working with the severely disabled can lead to feelings of coldness towards individuals and an intolerance of their inappropriate behaviours (Nind and Hewett 1998). The passivity of pupils with PMLD makes it relatively easy to introduce mainstream teaching methodologies that, in turn, reduce already fragile opportunities for teachers to interact co-actively and effectively with these pupils. Pupils with PMLD require teaching methodologies that have intensive interaction at their core (Nind and Hewett 1998) and that rely upon the ability of teachers to recognise and understand the idiosyncrasies of their pupils. SLD schools thus need to develop teaching methods that are properly supported by intimate knowledge of their pupils.

Another characteristic of pupils with SLD/PMLD that is known to impose emotional pressure upon teachers is the relatively high incidence of challenging behaviour (Kiernan and Kiernan 1994). Research has identified a long list of behaviours that teachers in these schools find particularly difficult to cope with (as adapted from the Mental Health Foundation 1997):

- physical aggression;
- self injury;
- shouting, swearing and making loud noises;
- distractibility and hyperactivity;
- obsessive and ritualistic behaviour;
- non-compliance and resistance to teaching.

From this long list of behaviours identified by Harris and colleagues (1986), physical aggression has been found to be one of the most intense for inflicting emotional pressure (Male and May 1997a, 1997b; Pimm 1998). Teachers employed in SLD schools have to work effectively with pupils who have behaviours that are notoriously difficult to manage and who are known to put staff under intense emotional pressure. However, it is unlikely that many SLD schools have been able to develop coherent and effective strategies for responding to the demands of pupils who have severe challenging behaviour. Although there has been some DfEE guidance about the management of violent behaviour (DfEE 1998c), there has also been increasing pressure upon schools to exclude pupils who require frequent use of physical restraint in order to control their aggression (NUT 2000).

Recent research has shown that, while teachers in SLD schools are likely to produce carefully written lesson plans describing how they intend to teach curriculum subjects, they are less likely to produce plans of a similar quality in response to severely challenging behaviour (Harris *et al.* 1996). Teachers have been described as showing anger, disgust and distress when having to cope with aspects of severe challenging behaviour; they have also been found to be overwhelmed by the extreme emotional pressures that result from it (Mental Health Foundation 1997). Teachers find themselves increasingly under pressure to either contain the aggression of their pupils or request that the most demanding pupils are accommodated elsewhere.

Having to cope with an increasing population of pupils with PMLD in the same school as pupils with severe challenging behaviour often leads to complaints from parents. These complaints centre around the fear of assault upon more vulnerable children and/or concern that, in order to contain the aggression of pupils who challenge the school organisation, time is detracted from profoundly disabled pupils (Mental Health Foundation 1997). Teachers who find themselves in such difficult situations can feel isolated and have been found to be unlikely to expect any real help from outside agencies (Harris *et al.* 1996), despite the multi-agency nature of SLD schools. The sense of isolation that teachers feel is also often shared by the parents of the pupils (Kiernan and Qureshi 1993). Although there is a common view that multi-agency strategies are required for coping with pupils with severe challenging behaviour, such multi-agency support is often found to be uncoordinated, typified by different agencies who undertake repeated specialist assessments but only rarely provide evidence of effective treatment regimes (Mental Health Foundation 1997).

Coping with the burden of emotional pressures no doubt contributes to the difficulties that some SLD schools experience when seeking to recruit and retain teachers. There are emotional pressures that are innate to working with pupils with SLD/PMLD. These pressures contribute to the frustrations that teachers in SLD schools have expressed at their lack of training in the education and care of pupils with SLD/PMLD (McNicholas 2000). The pressures also make a travesty of the generic systems that have been imposed upon SLD schools for appraising teacher effectiveness.

Staff who work with teachers in SLD schools

There is a wide range of staff who work alongside teachers in SLD schools, the most common of whom are TAs employed directly by the schools. The levels of qualification, along with the roles and responsibilities of TAs, varies significantly across the country, added to which few TAs have access to specialist training in the education and care of pupils with SLD/PMLD (Farrell *et al.* 1999). There are also large numbers of other staff who are employed by other service providers. As part of a team-building exercise undertaken in 1998, a case study example demonstrated that a pupil in an SLD school could be receiving services from as many as 25 different professionals (Aird 2000a), giving SLD schools an important multi-agency function to fulfil.

Of the staff who work in SLD schools, it has been found that TAs probably have the most difficult work situation to cope with (Aird 2000a). TAs have little authority in teacher-dominated classroom environments and are often directed to carry out specific educational, caring and treatment strategies with individual pupils. As a consequence of working individually with pupils, TAs tend to have an intimate knowledge of individual pupils and good levels of understanding about strategies that are effective for meeting their idiosyncratic needs. There can be little doubt that the TA role is an important one, but it is not always the case that the potential benefits of deploying TAs in the classroom are fully realised in practice. For example, when the role of the TA is either unclear and/or is not empowered appropriately, then the benefits of employing TAs are not maximised and these staff tend only to duplicate the work of the teacher (Jerwood 1999) rather than provide the highly specialised support roles that the needs of some pupils demand.

The relationship between teachers and TAs is critical for helping to ensure the effectiveness of a school's provision for pupils with SLD/PMLD. However, despite a long history of employing relatively large numbers of TAs in SLD schools, it is only quite recently that the nature of the teacher–TA relationship has had the attention of authoritative bodies such as the DfEE. For instance, it was only in 1997 that the DfEE declared its interest in the role of the TA, together with TA management and training, in the Green Paper entitled *Excellence for All Children: Meeting Special Educational Needs* (DfEE 1997). The DfEE went on to add further comment about the need to develop effective TA practice in its 1998 publication entitled *Meeting Special Educational Needs: A Programme of Action* (DfEE 1998a) and then again in the Green Paper *Teachers Meeting the Challenge of Change* (DfEE 1998b). This interest was followed up by the commissioning of a research study from the Centre for Educational Needs, University of Manchester, and subsequent publication of that study's findings in 1999 (Farrell *et al.* 1999). There can be little doubt that this recent interest in the work of TAs came about primarily because of the rapid increase in the number of TAs being employed to support the inclusion of pupils with SEN in mainstream schools (DfEE 1998b).

It is possible that the DfEE's interest in the role of TAs and their relationship with teachers will result in some form of generic accredited training and career structure being established (Aird 2000a). This opportunity needs to be capitalised upon if SLD schools are going to benefit. There is an urgent need to introduce specialist training for both teachers and TAs in SLD schools and, just as importantly, the multi-agency function of these schools needs to be improved.

The Department of Health (DoH) and the DfEE have both directed increasing attention towards the need for collaborative planning between specialist agencies. For example, in 1999 the DfEE published its guidance booklet, the *National Healthy School Standard* (DfEE 1999a), which was followed by the creation of a new Standards Fund category to help fund initiatives in inter-agency collaboration. Shortcomings in the quality of inter-agency collaboration have been known for a good number of years and influenced the content of the Children Act 1989. The proposal to establish local registers of children with disabilities was a key feature of the 1989 Act, and it was intended that these disability registers would become a disabled child's passport to well-coordinated multi-agency support. However, the registers have never been effectively realised in practice and the 1989 Act failed to secure collaborative inter-agency working, in much the same way as the Disabled Persons Act 1986 failed to ensure that the needs of disabled children were properly addressed in the home (Morris 1995).

In 1997, the SCAA advocated that other professionals, in addition to teachers, should be involved in curriculum development for pupils with SEN. A number of years previously, research had shown that it was unusual for inter-agency collaborations to be undertaken in the area of curriculum development, despite the fact that professionals from different disciplines often worked together in multi-agency environments such as SLD schools (Lacey and Lomas 1993). A study by Graham

(1995) suggested that, when teachers and therapists collaborated together, there were gains to be made on both sides. Without such collaborations, it was more likely that there would be enmity between professionals and a poorer quality of curriculum resulting for the pupils (McCaul 2000).

Despite the statements made about the need for multi-agency collaboration in the education of pupils with SEN (SCAA 1997b), little appears to have changed. Caring regimes, therapies and treatments continue to operate alongside the whole curriculum, sometimes undertaken by qualified staff from local health authorities, but often undertaken by TAs (Aird 2000a). Where therapies and medical treatments are undertaken by TAs, pupils receive their treatments at the hands of staff who are unlikely to be qualified in either the education of pupils with SLD/PMLD or in the treatments they are asked to undertake. The use of TAs in this manner introduces a third variable in the complex problem posed by the need for inter-agency collaboration in the SLD school.

Pupils with PMLD, in particular, have been shown to require a curriculum that needs to be delivered by a multi-agency team, as opposed to delivery by just one faction, be it teachers or their assistants (McCaul 2000). All members of a school's multi-agency team should be able to work effectively together in the delivery of the whole curriculum and should have shared ownership of the specialist features of that curriculum (Lawton 1996). However, because a curriculum is generally considered to be the province of teachers, the prospect for securing a whole curriculum that is multi-agency by design and function is remote, unless there are drastic changes introduced to the way in which SLD schools are organised.

The way forward may well lie in the manner in which the roles and responsibilities of TAs are organised. The 1999 report on the management, role and training of learning support assistants (Farrell *et al.* 1999) noted that TAs employed in SLD schools and those schools catering for children with autism were more likely to be involved in meetings relating to an Annual Review of SEN and to contribute to the planning and implementation of pupils' IEPs than were TAs employed in other types of school. From this evidence it may be assumed that TAs in SLD schools have increased opportunities for acquiring specific knowledge about the needs of their pupils beyond those of TAs in other sectors of education.

TAs who are employed in SLD schools have increasingly been expected to provide medical treatments and therapies for their pupils, as well as perform some teaching tasks (Blandford *et al.* 1998), and they have had to learn about administering therapies and treatments anecdotally during the course of carrying out their other duties. In some ways, the changing role of TAs in SLD schools has mirrored that of nurses. In the nursing profession, nurses have been expected to take on some of the responsibilities traditionally reserved for doctors – for instance, the prescribing of some medicines (DoH 1999). However, changes in nursing practice have been supported by accredited research-based training, in preference to staff having to learn about changes in their duties via experiential training (Autar 1996). Also, in response to the changing role of nurses, grading systems were introduced to operate alongside accredited training, in recognition of the varying levels of knowledge required for duties that overlap with the role of doctors. A similar strategy needs to be introduced into SLD schools, to help govern the role of TAs and improve effective inter-agency collaboration.

Increasingly, teachers have found it necessary to review the role of TAs in the classroom and reappraise how their careful deployment may be able to enhance special provision for their pupils (Jerwood 1999). Given the relatively low levels of pay, lack of career opportunities, increasing responsibilities and minimal authority that the majority of TAs in SLD schools command (Aird 2000a), fulfilling such a changing role may prove to be very difficult. A career structure for TAs needs to be established that provides a clear framework for undertaking educational and paramedical responsibilities. The role and responsibilities of TAs needs to be properly defined and empowered via incremental salary levels that are comple-mented with entry qualifications and performance criteria. Such a structure has already been established for TAs working in Coventry SLD schools, where a career structure has been linked to accredited training and entry-level qualifications (Aird 2000a).

The report entitled *The Management, Role and Training of Learning Support Assistants* (Farrell *et al.* 1999), advised that many of the accredited LEA/Further Education College courses that had been designed for TAs had been found to be lacking in appropriate content and often showed a disparity between what was taught on these courses and the demands of the tasks that TAs were required to undertake. This disparity was one of the reasons why *The Modular Course in the Education and Care of Children with Severe, Profound and Complex Learning Disabilities* (Aird 2000c) was developed for TAs employed by Coventry LEA.

The Modular Course was the result of close collaboration between teachers and professionals from a variety of agencies. The training that Coventry TAs receive via that course incorporates evidence-based research about the education, care and treatment of pupils with SLD/PMLD and combines theoretical training with reflective work-practice. The course is accredited by University College Worcester and is made up of 12 modules of study, leading to an award of a BA (Ed) degree. The first six modules, which lead to the award of a diploma, provide a specific focus on disability, including study on the topics of:

- severe challenging behaviour;
- acute autistic spectrum disorder;
- motor disorder;
- sensory and perceptual impairment;
- speech and language difficulties;
- life-threatening health difficulties;
- eating and drinking disorders;
- inter-agency collaboration;
- parent partnership;
- whole-curriculum issues;
- numeracy and literacy for pupils with SLD/PMLD;
- a statutory framework for the management of SEN.

The remaining six modules are research-based and are of a more generic nature. This second half of the course is designed to assist TAs, and/or teachers in obtaining an initial degree in the education and care of pupils with SLD/PMLD and thus to go some way towards making up for the deficit in initial specialist teacher-training.

Linked closely with the structure of this part-time modular course is a career structure that enables TAs to benefit from enhanced salaries in return for increased responsibility. Further collaboration between the authority's SLD schools and the local authority's Healthcare (National Health Service, NHS) Trust is aiming to secure the provision of jointly funded posts. Joint funding is being proposed for TAs who have gained their national diploma, in recognition of the multi-agency function they will be required to undertake. Planning is currently under way to merge the management of *The Modular Course* with specialist training provided by the local Healthcare (NHS) Trust, to further cement the spirit of multi-agency collaboration.

The creation of a tier of highly trained TAs who are empowered to provide a quasi-teaching/medical role mirrors that of the para-educator developed in the USA (Morgan *et al.* 1998). The role of the para-educator was developed to fill the ideological gap that existed between teachers and medical staff in schools for disabled children. The potential for a para-educator role of this type attracted the attention of the Warnock Committee during the late 1970s (Warnock DES 1978) and was further elaborated upon in the early 1990s (Orelove and Sobsey 1993). In recent years, however, the role of the para-educator has not received anywhere near the extent of national attention that it deserves, and now is the time for the debate to be resurrected.

There may be purists who advocate that the provision of treatments and therapeutic, caring regimes are the responsibility of the DoH and that local health authorities ought to employ sufficient numbers of therapists and paramedical staff to service the needs of pupils with SLD/PMLD. However, such views are narrow-minded, unrealistic and contrary to what is known about a child's needs for comfort and security. Invasive treatments and intimate caring regimes are surely best undertaken by staff whom pupils know and trust the best. Those staff, in SLD schools, are likely to be TAs, who already have good holistic knowledge of their pupils' needs and who are probably familiar in acquiring specialist advice from supporting professionals in an anecdotal way. It would be far better to formalise and rationalise current ad-hoc arrangements than risk confusing the multi-agency function of SLD schools any further.

An insistence that therapies and treatments are carried out solely by supporting agencies would result in pupils being subjected to invasive handling by a large number of comparative strangers who, although possessing expert clinical knowledge about an aspect of a pupil's disability, lack the holistic knowledge that TAs tend to hold. Governors and head teachers need to look to how the traditional role of school staff can be modified so as to improve the quality of the holistic care and treatment of their pupils. Although the modification of staff roles in the SLD school might be difficult to achieve, it is neither an unreasonable request to make of SLD schools nor an unrealistic expectation for them to achieve (Lacey and Lomas 1993).

A question of leadership

The leadership of an SLD school is a distinctly complex and demanding occupation that incorporates the responsibility of whole-school management (Handy 1993). The process of managing a school is generally considered to be the responsibility and preserve of the head teacher, together with a small number of senior staff to whom managerial responsibilities are delegated. However, the management of pupils with SLD/PMLD is far too important a task to be left to just a small team of senior teachers who are considered to be leaders. All staff who are involved in collaborative activities are required to act as managers to a varying degree, and leaders are needed at all levels (Eraut 1994). Individual members of staff need to be empowered within the multi-agency function of SLD schools and enabled to manage specific aspects of specialist provision, in collaboration with other key players.

Unfortunately, there are no national guidelines available, currently, to advise SLD schools about how best to organise the individual responsibilities of teachers, TAs and supporting professionals. This lack of guidance is not helpful for securing effective inter-agency collaboration and, as such, pupils with SLD/PMLD are not benefiting as well as they might from the multi-agency function of their host schools. This is a situation that needs to change if SLD schools wish to see improving standards of education, care and treatment. Structures need to be agreed and put in place so that the multi-agency function of SLD schools can be properly realised. Figure 7.1 illustrates how an SLD school might consider defining the roles and responsibilities of different professionals, and how it might negotiate funding arrangements with the local health authority.

Roles, responsibilities and the management of staff performance

Teachers in SLD schools require specialist training if they are to do their job appropriately. In addition to a proper understanding of disability, teachers in SLD schools also need meaningful guidance about specialist teaching methods that are appropriate to the education and care of pupils with SLD/PMLD. In order for standards in the education and care of these pupils to be raised, the performance of all staff who provide services to pupils with SLD/PMLD needs to be considered. Legislation on the performance management of teachers (DfEE 2000a) represents an ideal opportunity for SLD schools to establish systems with which to raise standards of education and care. However, singling out the performance management of teachers, in isolation from other categories of staff, is simply not sufficient to raise standards on a whole-school basis.

SLD schools need to consider the recommendations illustrated in Figure 7.1, tease out the actual duties and responsibilities inherent within each position within each particular school's context, and agree how the performance of staff in each of these categories is to be managed. A school needs to have a clear and coherent overview of the responsibilities of each professional and also a shared understanding of how these responsibilities come together, in order to provide suitable setting conditions for the education, care and treatment of individual pupils. Such clear, shared understanding would provide the criteria for appraising the performance of all staff. Without shared criteria of this type, school managers – at whatever level – would be unable to guarantee the setting conditions necessary for pupils to learn effectively (Bull and Solity 1987). When the roles and responsibilities of different categories of staff are properly identified and empowered within

School-funded posts

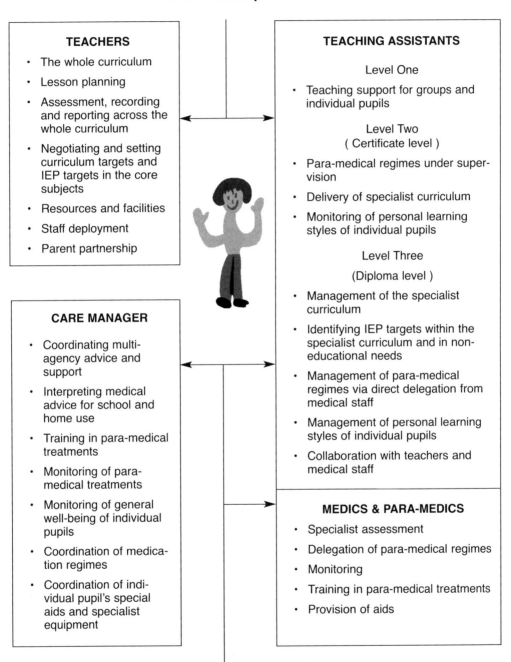

TEACHERS

- The whole curriculum
- Lesson planning
- Assessment, recording and reporting across the whole curriculum
- Negotiating and setting curriculum targets and IEP targets in the core subjects
- Resources and facilities
- Staff deployment
- Parent partnership

TEACHING ASSISTANTS

Level One

- Teaching support for groups and individual pupils

Level Two
(Certificate level)

- Para-medical regimes under supervision
- Delivery of specialist curriculum
- Monitoring of personal learning styles of individual pupils

Level Three

(Diploma level)

- Management of the specialist curriculum
- Identifying IEP targets within the specialist curriculum and in non-educational needs
- Management of para-medical regimes via direct delegation from medical staff
- Management of personal learning styles of individual pupils
- Collaboration with teachers and medical staff

CARE MANAGER

- Coordinating multi-agency advice and support
- Interpreting medical advice for school and home use
- Training in para-medical treatments
- Monitoring of para-medical treatments
- Monitoring of general well-being of individual pupils
- Coordination of medication regimes
- Coordination of individual pupil's special aids and specialist equipment

MEDICS & PARA-MEDICS

- Specialist assessment
- Delegation of para-medical regimes
- Monitoring
- Training in para-medical treatments
- Provision of aids

Health authority-funded and jointly funded posts

Figure 7.1 Roles and responsibilities in the SLD school

the multi-agency function of SLD schools, the imposition of secondary motivational handicaps (Seligman 1975) is less likely to come about.

It should not be impossible for SLD schools, in partnership with other service providers, to agree a common framework for managing the performance of staff who contribute to the multi-agency function of SLD schools. There can be no justification for seeking to perpetuate a system of multi-agency functioning that has been found to be uncoordinated and that rarely provides evidence of effective treatment regimes (Mental Health Foundation 1997). Working as part of a complex multi-agency team brings its own pressures and demands for special aptitudes (Roberts 1994). The willingness and ability of individual staff to share personal expertise, provide mutual support, plan collaboratively and, where occasion demands, exchange roles for a period of time, have all been described as being essential for effective teamwork (Wright and Kersner 1998). There is also a plethora of work-practice skills that are necessary for good collaboration to occur between different professionals. The skills of assertiveness, negotiation, consultation and reflection have all been identified as being essential for effective multi-agency collaboration in the SLD school (Aird 2000a).

All of these aptitudes need to be brought together into a single system for managing the performance of staff in SLD schools, regardless of which agency is actually funding the salary of particular staff members. Performance management does not have to be the sole preserve of a school's SMT. The best systems for managing staff performance are those in which reflective work-practice features highly and in which members of staff, at all levels, are empowered to provide a managerial role in the appraisal of colleagues in the workplace (West and Ainscow 1991).

In order for performance management to be successful, there needs to be a commitment to a set of guiding principles, shared between an SLD school and its service providers. Such principles might include (DfEE 2000a, adapted) a shared commitment to:

- an emphasis on monitoring the quality of everyday practice;
- providing access to relevant, effective and accredited training;
- guaranteeing staff expertise at levels that are appropriate for carrying out specific teaching techniques, caring regimes, therapies and treatments;
- providing opportunities for all staff to progress within their chosen career and/or to transfer to related career paths;
- an emphasis upon professional reflection and self-review;
- performance-management arrangements that will enable staff to achieve their

potential through agreeing objectives and having their performance assessed by an unbiased reviewer.

Analysis of local authority expenditure is likely to reveal that approximately 80 per cent of all expenditure on disabled children is taken up by staffing costs. When considered on a regional scale, society invests a huge amount of public money in the staffing of different service providers to ensure that good provision is made for its disabled children. In order to ensure good value for money on a regional basis, it is important that SLD schools and local agencies agree a shared system for managing the multi-agency performance of their staff. It is recommended that a portfolio approach is used to provide this common system, and that SLD schools are charged with the responsibility of managing such a system because of the inherent multi-agency function of these schools.

The portfolio approach

SLD schools are complex, multi-agency environments in which professionals from a variety of disciplines need to be able to collaborate and work together effectively. In order for school provision to be effective, individual members of staff need to be able to demonstrate their personal awareness of what has been called organisational effectiveness (Carlson 1967). Tests of organisational effectiveness may be gained from judging how well each member of a school's extended staff is aware of that school's basic structures. These include (West and Ainscow 1991, adapted):

- standards that govern the quality of duties expected of each category of staff;
- lines of authority that indicate to which managers different categories of staff are accountable and for what;
- opportunities for progression within a particular category of staffing, and opportunities that might occur for staff to transfer between categories;
- the relationships that are expected of different staff when collaborating in the delivery of holistic provision;
- systems for encouraging maximum executive performance of individual staff.

When staff are required to maintain a personal portfolio, it is possible to use this resource as the basis for performance management. A portfolio does not need to be an expensively produced document. A loose-leaf ring binder, divided into sections, can provide an excellent portfolio for organising the performance management of staff. Proposed contents for such a personal portfolio are set out next.

Section 1: Personal statement

The first section of a portfolio can be used for staff to describe their personal understanding of their role, responsibilities and how their individual function fits into the school's philosophical and organisational framework. Analysis of the information recorded in Section 1 would illustrate how well individual staff understand a school's organisational structures and value their own role within such a structure. Staff ownership of a school's organisational framework is essential for enabling a healthy working environment to be fostered (Drucker 1955). Appraisal and analysis of what staff record within Section 1 of their portfolios is something that needs to be undertaken by a school's SMT. This information would be helpful for informing the school's programme of in-service training and for the dissemination of the school's philosophy, organisation and SDP.

However, other aspects of performance management, as managed via the appraisal of staff portfolios, need not demand the time and immediate attention of the SMT. Performance management can be undertaken by those staff who are deemed to be in the best position to:

- make meaningful, constructive criticism about the provision of specific teaching, caring, therapeutic and treatment duties by different categories of staff;
- overview the work and ability of staff who are to be reviewed;
- provide appropriate levels of support to the staff being reviewed.

A school will need to identify which staff are in the best position to undertake performance management, according to analysis of these three criteria. Other sections of the portfolio can then be organised and appraised.

Section 2: Personal plan

In Section 2, staff should build upon their interpretation of the school's organisational framework by recording how they would like to improve their own performance. This section is intended to foster the skill of reflective work practice that is important for whole-school development (Shon 1983). Information of this type might include:

- identification of key issues and/or SDP priorities that individual staff particularly identify with, and suggestions how staff would like to see these whole-school priorities progressed;
- long-term professional aspirations;

- an action plan of what the member of staff believes he or she needs to do in order to achieve those long-term aspirations;
- proposed short-term objectives that the member of staff believes can be addressed over the course of the first year of performance management.

Individual staff members may also wish to include information that represents concerns they have about whole-school issues that they believe might inhibit their progress. Information of this type might include:

- issues that the individual member of staff believes limits the ability to fulfil his or her role effectively and/or gain job satisfaction;
- reference to how aspects of the school's ethos and/or organisation might be constraining the development of collaborative practice, multi-agency function and/or the raising of standards generally;
- how short-term objectives or long-term career aspirations might be constrained by the school's current organisation.

Completion of Section 2 should trigger the first meeting between the reviewer and the member of staff whose performance is to be appraised. Ideally, a reviewer should be able to observe the member of staff carrying out particular duties, although for various reasons it may not be possible to observe all staff in practical situations. However, it is possible for video recordings to be used, in place of direct observation, and the use of such videos has been found to be valuable in assisting in staff appraisal (Hopkins 1985). Video recordings of the work of therapists, nurses, doctors and other specialists in the school setting would be particularly helpful for appraising the multi-agency function of SLD schools. For teachers, classroom observation is part of the statutory requirement for their performance management, and the OFSTED framework for observing the work of teachers is recommended for this purpose (DfEE 2000a).

Where possible, it is recommended that classroom observation is undertaken for both teachers and TAs. Suggested criteria to assist in the appraisal of teachers and TAs – felt to be more relevant to SLD schools than some of the OFSTED criteria – are described later in this chapter. These criteria are deliberately focused upon the management of setting conditions, an area of critical importance in the education and care of pupils with SLD/PMLD.

Section 3: The initial performance-management meeting

During the initial performance-management meeting, the reviewer needs to appraise information that staff have recorded in Sections 1 and 2 of the portfolio. Before agreeing a date for this initial meeting, a reviewer needs to ensure feedback has occurred from the SMT concerning Section 1 information. This feedback is necessary for enabling staff to improve their understanding of the whole-school organisational framework.

The focus of this initial meeting, however, is to consider the draft performance objectives that the member of staff being appraised has proposed for the coming year. Analysis from the observation of classroom practice, or from video recordings of everyday practice, should be used to encourage reflective work practice, to emphasise the importance of setting conditions, and to refine multi-agency functioning.

A list of three performance objectives should be determined for the coming year and agreed between the reviewer and the member of staff being appraised. Ideally, these objectives should include reference to the following areas:

- any particular weakness a staff member might be facing in carrying out his or her basic duties and/or maintaining setting conditions that are empathetic to the personal learning styles of pupils;
- objectives that reflect whole-school priorities for raising the standards of education and care of pupils;
- skills that will improve multi-agency collaboration and the multi-agency function of the school.

Once objectives have been agreed, the reviewer should then also negotiate what support the staff member might require in order to achieve their objectives. This information needs to be recorded and might include access to:

- in-service training;
- work shadowing and/or mentoring;
- reference materials;
- membership of particular steering groups and working parties.

Before concluding the initial performance-management meeting, the reviewer should identify the kinds of evidence that the staff member might like to gather during the course of the coming year, in order to demonstrate their subsequent progress within performance objectives. Evidence of this nature might include:

- demonstrable evidence of pupil progress;
- evidence of changes in other people and in their role, as a consequence of actions taken by the staff member;
- changes in the staff member's competency to do his or her job, demonstrable by evidence of record keeping, lesson planning, care plans etc.;
- changes made to the way in which classroom environments are organised;
- any literature that the staff member may produce or use to inform their developing practice;
- details of any training, mentoring or work shadowing that has been undertaken, and a description of how this knowledge has been used to improve personal work practice;
- minutes of any meetings that are felt to be relevant.

At the end of the performance-management meeting, the objectives that have been agreed should be written up, together with any relevant plans for giving the staff member access to training etc. Copies should be retained by both the reviewer and the staff member being appraised. A copy should also be forwarded to the SMT for inclusion in the SDP. Any information that is critical to the school's organisation and/or ethos also needs to be referred back to the SMT for action and/or dissemination to the managers of other service providers.

Section 4: Evidence of progress within performance targets
In this final section of the portfolio, the staff member should collate any evidence felt to be relevant to demonstrating progress within the personal performance objectives. It is this kind of empirical evidence, together with evidence from observed practice, that will provide input to the second and subsequent performance-management meetings. Staff should be encouraged to be reflective when gathering evidence of their progress, and to describe how their work-practice skills have changed as a consequence of actions they have taken.

Suggested criteria for appraising the performance of teachers and TAs

Schools will need to think carefully about the criteria they will use for appraising the performance of their teachers and TAs. Although the DfEE identified criteria for the performance management of teachers (DfEE 2000a), these criteria are generic. There are aspects of the education and care of pupils with SLD/PMLD that are peculiar to the SLD sector and that are particularly important for effective multi-agency working. Staff in SLD schools may find the following sets of criteria helpful when observing teachers and TAs at work in the classroom.

Criteria relating to the performance management of teachers

Multi-agency function

- Regular opportunities are organised for consultation with support staff and other key personnel in order to share holistic knowledge about pupils.
- Delegation is used to empower support staff in the delivery of the specialist curriculum.
- Regular communications are maintained with parents of all pupils.
- Skills of consultation and negotiation are used to assist with teamworking.
- Good time-management skills and the ability to meet deadlines are demonstrated.
- There is a sense of personal accountability.

Teaching technique

- Good discipline is maintained in the classroom.
- All pupils are engaged in meaningful activities at an appropriate level.
- Activities are delivered with good humour and are motivating.
- New activities and skills are introduced via good modelling.
- Pupils and support staff are clearly directed in their tasks.
- Delivery of lessons is empathetic to the learning style of individual pupils.
- The language of tuition is succinct and supported by total communication strategies.
- Pupils are prompted appropriately.
- Rewards and sanctions are used appropriately.
- Task analysis is employed to enable learning.
- Lessons have a clear activity focus, with a good structure and with opportunities for individual and group work.

Teacher responsibilities

- Teacher files are maintained in line with exemplar materials.
- Information about pupils is maintained in line with exemplar materials.
- Lesson planning is systematic, has a clear educational focus, describes differentiated activities for individual pupils, and directs the deployment of staff and teaching resources appropriately.

- The monitoring of pupil performance is undertaken in a systematic manner and information is recorded appropriately.
- Record keeping is used in a formative way to inform teaching.
- Reports are objective, clearly written and informative.
- Targets for the core subjects (English and Communication, Mathematics and ICT) are set appropriately, and they are organised for both discreet and cross-curricular delivery.
- IEP targets are set appropriately for subjects of the specialist curriculum, and they are organised for both discreet and cross-curricular delivery.
- Systems are in place to manage support-staff responsibilities.
- The classroom is organised according to needs of pupils, is tidy and is fit for purpose.
- Timetable commitments are honoured.

Whole-school responsibilities
- Subject policy, Key Stage plans and Schemes of Work (SoW) are fit for purpose, up to date and monitored in order to keep subject frameworks dynamic.
- Subject resources are maintained at a suitable level, are accessible and are managed effectively.
- Other staff are kept well informed about the organisation of subjects via in-service training and/or guidance notes.
- Networks are established with advisory services and other schools in order to maintain effectiveness of subject policy and practice.
- Opportunities are organised for consultation on quality and effectiveness of subject materials.

Criteria relating to the performance management of teaching assistants

Multi-agency function
- TAs have confidence to contribute to planning meetings.
- There is a willingness and ability to organise meetings with teachers, parents and support staff as necessary.
- Skills of consultation and negotiation are used to assist with effective team-building.
- An ability is shown to provide an advocacy role on behalf of pupils.
- There is a willingness to be accountable for personal responsibilities.
- Good time-management skills and ability to meet deadlines are demonstrated.

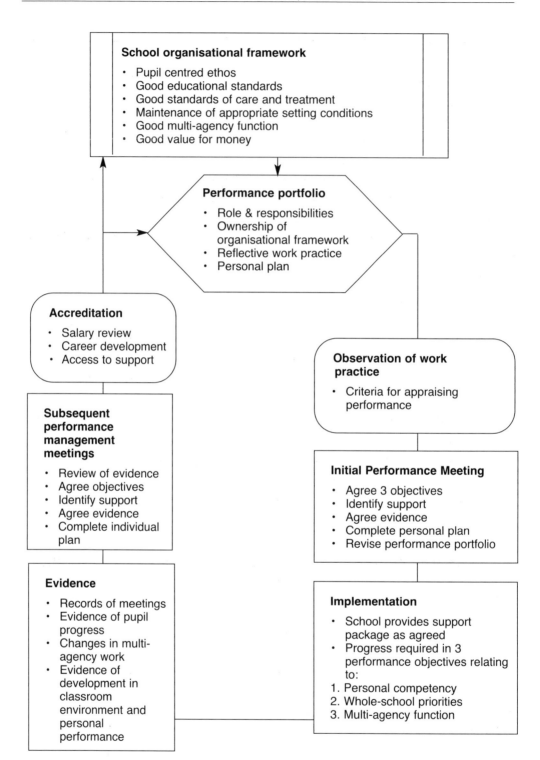

Figure 7.2 The use of portfolios as a method of linking whole-school development with multi-agency staff performance management

Teaching function
- A willingness is shown to work with individual pupils and with small groups.
- TAs engage pupils in meaningful activities at an appropriate level.
- Activities are delivered with good humour and are motivating.
- Activities and new skills are introduced via good modelling.
- Pupils are clearly directed in their tasks.
- One-to-one work is empathetic to the learning style of individual pupils.
- The language used is succinct and supported by total communication strategies.
- Pupils are prompted appropriately.
- Rewards and sanctions are used appropriately.
- Task analysis is employed to enable learning.

Specialist function
- Specialist support files are maintained in line with exemplar materials.
- Pupil information is maintained in line with exemplar materials and includes coherent descriptions of the personal learning styles of pupils for whom the TA is responsible.
- Suggestions for IEP targets are based on the objective assessment of pupils against the specialist curriculum and endorsed with advice from support services as necessary.
- There is demonstrable knowledge about the content of the specialist curriculum and an ability to teach activities incorporated within subject curricula.
- Resources for the specialist curriculum are maintained in good order.
- Opportunities are organised for collaboration with support services, parents and other sources of expert advice in order to gather information about pupils.
- The monitoring of pupil progress is objective and record keeping is accurate.
- There is demonstrable knowledge of therapeutic, treatment and caring regimes and an ability to provide services discreetly and with respect for the pupil's feelings.
- The aspirations and feelings of pupils are advocated to teachers and other staff as necessary.

Figure 7:2 Illustrates the use of portfolios as a method of linking whole-school development with multi-agency staff performance management.

Concluding comments

The effective education and care of pupils with SLD/PMLD, regardless of how slight or severe an individual pupil's disabilities might be, demands harmonious multi-agency function (Kershaw 1974). If individual members of staff are secure in their role, then they are more likely to be able to function effectively as part of a multi-agency team (Fish 1985). It makes good sense, therefore, for an SLD school to invest heavily in the management of all categories of staff who contribute to the education and care of pupils with SLD/PMLD. If the performance of staff in an SLD school is managed properly, then it follows that the subsequent learning environment will be conducive to developing high-quality provision for the education, care and treatment of its pupils.

There are a number of factors that should be kept in mind when seeking to perfect the ideal learning environment. The multi-agency staff of an SLD school need to:

- have clear roles and responsibilities;
- be empowered in their roles and responsibilities;
- have opportunities to collaborate, plan together and learn from one another;
- have the knowledge, skills and understanding necessary to undertake their basic duties;
- have clearly defined systems for monitoring their performance.

One final factor needs to be added to this list, without which the problem of trying to create the optimum learning environment for pupils with SLD/PMLD cannot easily be resolved. That one factor is clarity of purpose. An SLD school must have great clarity regarding the needs of its pupils and regarding the demands that the personal learning styles of those pupils impose upon the staff who are to educate, care for and treat them. The problem facing SLD schools is how to provide their pupils with as much expert knowledge and consistency of environment as possible (Brown *et al.* 1998) while at the same time engaging them in a curriculum that is suitably broad, balanced and appropriate to their needs. There is no esoteric 'holy grail' that head teachers need to pursue in order to realise the rights, needs and aspirations of their pupils. To use a famous but often misinterpreted quote: 'Pupils with special needs do not need integration. What they need is education.' (Hegarty *et al.* 1982)

Unambiguous, effective whole-school management is the key to providing and sustaining the educational provision and care that pupils with SLD/PMLD require and deserve in order for them to flourish.

References

Aird, R. (2000a) 'The case for specialist training for learning support assistants employed in schools for children with severe, profound and multiple learning difficulties', *Support for Learning* **15**(3), 106–10.

Aird, R. (2000b) 'Teaching English and literacy to pupils with severe, profound and multiple learning difficulties', *British Journal of Special Education*, **27** (4). 171–75.

Aird, R. and Heath, S. (2000) 'The teaching of English and literacy to secondary aged pupils with profound and multiple learning difficulties, *PMLD Link* **12**(1), 15–18.

Aird, R. and Bainbridge, S. (1997) 'Whole School Management: Turning an illusion into practice', *British Journal of Special Education,* **24**(1), 12–17.

Aird, R. and Lister, J. (1999) 'Enhancing provision for pupils with autism in a school for pupils with severe learning difficulties', *Good Autism Practice,* April 1999, 17–25.

Aitken, S. and Buultjens, M. (1992) *Vision for Doing. Assessing Functional Vision of Learners who are Multiple Disabled.* Edinburgh: Moray House Publications.

Audit Commission and Her Majesty's Inspectorate of Education (1992a) *Getting in on the Act. Provision for Pupils with Special Educational Needs: The National Picture.* London: HMSO.

Audit Commission and Her Majesty's Inspectorate of Education (1992b) *Getting the Act Together. A Handbook for Schools and Local Education Authorities.* London: HMSO.

Autar, R. (1996) 'Role of the nurse teacher in advanced nursing practice', *British Journal of Nursing* **5**(5), 298–301.

Bainbridge, S. (1999) 'The implementation of the National Literacy Strategy in schools for children with severe, profound and multiple learning difficulties', *The SLD Experience* **23**, Spring 1999, 5–6.

Barnardos (1995) *Disabled Children and Legislation: No. 3 Education and the Disabled Child.* London: Barnardos.

Banes, D. (1999) *Spiral Mathematics: Progression and Continuity in Mathematics for Pupils Working Towards Level 1.* Tamworth: NASEN.

Barber, B. and Goldbart, J. (1998) 'Accounting for learning and failure to learn in people with profound and multiple learning disabilities', in Lacey, P. and Ouvry, C. (eds) *People with Profound and Multiple Learning Disabilities.* London: David Fulton Publishers.

Blandford, S. *et al.* (1998) 'A survey of training and professional development for learning support assistants', *Support for Learning* **13**(4), 179–84.

Booth, T. *et al.* (2000) *Index for Inclusion.* Bristol: CSIE.

Bradley, A. (1998) 'Community based rehabilitation in developing countries' in Lacey, P. and Ouvry, C. (eds) *People with Profound and Multiple Learning Disabilities: A Collaborative Approach to Meeting Complex Needs.* London: David Fulton Publishers.

Brennan, W. K. (1974) *Shaping the Education of Slow Learners.* London: Routledge and Kegan Paul.

Brown, E. (1996) *Religious Education for All.* London: David Fulton Publishers.

Brown, N. *et al.* (1998) 'Sensory Needs', in Lacey, P. and Ouvry, C. (eds) *People with Profound and Multiple Learning Disabilities.* London: David Fulton Publishers.

Brudenell, P. (1987) 'Dramatherapy with people with a mental handicap', in Jennings, S. (ed) *Dramatherapy: Theory and Practice for Teachers and Clinicians.* London: Croom Helm.

Bruner, J. (1975) 'The ontogenesis of speech acts', *Journal of Child Language* **2**, 1–19.

Bull, S.L. and Solity, J. E. (1987) *Classroom Management: Principles to Practice*. London: Croom Helm.

Bush, T. (1986) *Theories of Educational Management*. London: Harper and Row.

Byers, R. (1999) 'Experience and achievement: initiatives in curriculum development for pupils with severe, profound and multiple learning difficulties', *British Journal of Special Education* **26**(4), 184–8.

Byers, R. and Rose, R. (1994) 'Schools should decide …', in Rose, R., Fergusson, A., Coles, C., Byers, R. and Banes, D. (eds) *Implementing the Whole Curriculum for Pupils with Learning Difficulties*. London: David Fulton Publishers.

Byers, R. and Rose, R. (1996) *Planning the Curriculum for Pupils with Special Educational Needs: A Practical Guide*. London: David Fulton Publishers.

Carlson, D. (1967) *Modern Management*. Alhambra, CA: Tinnon-Brown.

Carpenter, B. (1990) 'Unlocking the door: access to English in the National Curriculum for children with severe learning difficulties', in Smith, B. *Interactive Approaches to Teaching the Core Subjects*. Bristol: Lame Duck Publishing.

Carpenter, B. and Ashdown, R. (1996) 'Enabling access', in Carpenter, B., Ashdown, R. and Bovair, K. *Enabling Access: Effective Teaching and Learning for Pupils with Learning Difficulties*. London: David Fulton Publishers.

Christ Church College (1996) *Final Report to the Department for Education: National Survey of Local Education Authorities, Policies and Procedures for the Identification of and Provision for Children who are out of School by Reason of Exclusion or Otherwise*. Canterbury: Christ Church College.

Coupe-O'Kane, J. and Goldbart, J. (1998) *Communication Before Speech: Development and Assessment*. London: David Fulton Publishers.

Dearing, Sir R. (1994) *The National Curriculum and its Assessment*. London: SCAA.

Department of Education and Science (1970) *Education (Handicapped Children) Act 1970*. London: HMSO

Department of Education and Science (1978) *Special Educational Needs: Report of the Committee of Enquiry into the Education of Handicapped Children and Young People* (The Warnock Report). London: HMSO

Department of Education and Science (1988) *Education Reform Act 1988*. London: HMSO.

Department of Education and Science (1989) *Planning for School Development: Advice to Governors, Headteachers and Teachers* (Hargreaves Report). London: HMSO.

Department for Education and Science (1989) Circular 22/89 *Assessment and Statements of Special Educational Need*. London: HMSO.

Department for Education (1993) *Education Act 1993*. London: Department for Education.

Department for Education (1994a) *Code of Practice on the Identification and Assessment of Special Educational Need*. London: Department for Education.

Department for Education (1994b) Circular 2/94 *Local Management of Schools*. London: Department for Education.

Department for Education and Employment (1997) *Excellence for All Children: Meeting Special Educational Needs*. London: DfEE.

Department for Education and Employment (1998a) *Meeting Special Educational Needs: A Programme of Action*. London: DfEE

Department for Education and Employment (1998b) *Teachers Meeting the Challenge of Change*. London: DfEE.

Department for Education and Employment (1998c) *The Use of Force to Control or Restrain Pupils*. London: DfEE.

Department for Education and Employment (1998d) *The National Literacy Strategy*. London: DfEE.

Department for Education and Employment (1999a) *The National Healthy School Standard*. London: DfEE.

Department for Education and Employment (1999b) *The National Numeracy Strategy: Framework for Teaching Mathematics*. Sudbury: DfEE Publications.

Department for Education and Employment (2000a) *Performance Management in Schools*. London: DfEE.

Department for Education and Employment (2000b) *SEN Code of Practice on the Identification and Assessment of Pupils with SEN Thresholds: Good Practice Guidance on Identification and Provision for Pupils with Special Educational Needs*, consultation document. London: DfEE.

Department of Health Social Services Inspectorate (1993) *Corporate Parents: Inspection of Residential Care Services in 11 Local Authorities*. London: Social Services Inspectorate, Department of Health.

Detheridge, T. and Detheridge, M. (1997) *Literacy Through Symbols: Improving Access for Cildren and Adults*. London: David Fulton Publishers.

Drucker, P. F. (1955) *The Practice of Management*. London: Heinemann.

Eraut, M. (1994) *Developing Professional Knowledge and Competence*. London: Falmer Press.

EQUALS (1998) *Baseline Assessment Scheme and Curriculum Target Setting*. Tyne and Wear: EQUALS.

Fagg, S. *et al.* (1990) *Entitlement For All in Practice*. London: David Fulton Publishers.

Farrell, P. *et al.* (1999) *The Management, Role and Training of Learning Support Assistants*. London: DfEE.

Filder, R. (1989) 'Background to the Education Reform Act', in Fidler, B. and Bowles, G. (eds) *Effective Local Management of Schools*. Harlow: BEMAS/Longman.

Field, T. (1977) 'Games parents play with normal and high risk infants', *Child Psychiatry and Infant Development,* **14**, 41–8.

Fish, J. (1985) *Educational Opportunities for All/The Report of the Committee Reviewing Provision to Meet Special Educational Needs (The Fish Report)*. London: ILEA.

Fish, J. (1989) *What is Special Education?*. Milton Keynes: Open University Press.

Foxen, T. and McBrien, J. (1981) *Training Staff in Behavioural Methods: Trainee Workbook*. Manchester: Manchester University Press.

Fuller, C. (1999) 'Bag books tactile stories', *The SLD Experience* **23**, Spring 1999, 20–1.

Gardner, H. (1984) *Frames of Mind: The Theory of Multiple Intelligence*. London: Heinemann.

Ganesh, S. *et al.* (1994) 'An audit of physical health needs of adults with profound learning disability in a hospital population', *Mental Handicap Research* **7**(3), 228–36.

Gilbert, C. (1992) 'Planning school development', in Booth, T., Swann, W., Masterton, M. and Potts, P. (eds) *Learning For All 2: Policies for Diversity In Education*. London: Routledge.

Goldbart, J. (1986) 'The development of language and communication', in Coupe, J. and Porter, J. (eds) *The Education of Children with Severe Learning Difficulties*. London: Croom Helm.

Goldsmith, J. and Goldsmith, L. (1998) 'Physical management', in Lacey, P. and Ouvry, C. (eds) *People with Profound and Multiple Learning Disabilities: A Collaborative Approach to Meeting Complex Needs*. London: David Fulton Publishers.

Graham, J. (1995) 'Inter-professional Collaboration in the Special School'. Unpublished PhD thesis. London: Institute of Education, University of London.

Graves, J. (2000) 'Vocabulary needs in augmentative and alternative communication: a sample of conversational topics between staff providing services to adults with learning difficulties and their service users', *British Journal of Learning Disabilities* **28**(3), 113–28.

Grove, N. and Peacey, N. (1999) 'Teaching subjects to pupils with profound and multiple learning difficulties', *British Journal of Special Education* **26**(2), 83–6.

Halpin, J. and Lewis, A. (1996) 'The impact of the National Curriculum on twelve special schools', *European Journal of Special Needs Education,* **11**, 95–105.

Handy, C. (1993) *Understanding Organisations*. London: Penguin.

Harris, J. (1994) Language, communication and personal power: a developmental perspective', in Coupe-O'Kane, J. and Smith, B. (eds) *Taking Control: Enabling People with Learning Difficulties*. London: David Fulton Publishers.

Harris, J. (1996) 'Physical restraint procedures for managing challenging behaviours presented by mentally retarded adults and children', *Research in Developmental Disabilities* **17**(2), 99–134.

Harris, J. *et al.* (1996) *Pupils with Severe Learning Difficulties who present Challenging Behaviour: A Whole School Approach to Assessment and Intervention*. Kidderminster: British Institute of Mental Handicap.

Harris, J. *et al.* (1996) *Physical Interventions: A Policy Framework*. London: British Institute of Learning Disabilities/National Autistic Society.

Harris, M. and Thompson, J. (2000) 'Lets do it! Numeracy at Hawkesbury Fields School', *The SLD Experience* **26**, Spring, 13–15.

Hawke, A. and Stanislawski, N. (1999) 'Personal passports: Hey!! It's all about me' **24**, Summer, 5–6.

Hegarty, S. *et al.* (1982) *Integration in Action: Case Studies of the Integration of Pupils with Special Needs*. Slough: NFER/Nelson.

Henderson, S.E. (1985) Motor development in Down's Syndrome', in Lane, D. and Stratford, B. (eds) *Current Approaches in Down's Syndrome*. Holt, Norfolk: Reinhart and Winston.

Hinchcliffe, V. (1996) 'English', in Carpenter, B., Ashdown, R. and Bovair, K. (eds) *Enabling Access: Effective Teaching and Learning for Pupils with Learning Difficulties*. London: David Fulton Publishers.

Hogg, J. (1982) 'Motor development and performance of severely mentally handicapped people', *Developmental Medicine and Child Neurology* **24**, 188–93.

Hogg, J. (1986) 'Motor competence in children with mental handicap', in Coupe, J. and Porter, J., *Education of Children with Severe Learning Difficulties*. London: Croom Helm.

Hopkins, D. (1985) *A Teacher's Guide to Classroom Practice*. Milton Keynes: Open University.

Humphrey, K. (1997) 'Voicing a curriculum debate for children with severe learning difficulties', in *EQUALS: Preview – Voicing Curriculum concerns*. Newcastle: University of Northumbria/EQUALS.

Hutchinson, C. (1998) 'Positive health: a collective responsibility', in Lacey, P. and Ouvry, C. (eds) *People with Profound and Multiple Learning Disabilities*. London: David Fulton Publishers.

Jerwood, L. (1999) 'Using special needs assistants effectively', *British Journal of Special Education* **26**(3), 127–9.

Johnson, D. W. and Johnson, F. P. (1987) *Joining Together: Group Theory and Group Skills*. Englewood Cliffs, New Jersey: Prentice Hall.

Jones, J. (2000)'Passports' to children with autism', *Good Autism Practice,* **1**(1), 56–62.

Kershaw, J. D. (1974) 'Handicapped children in the ordinary school', in Boswell, D. M. and Wingrove, J. M. (eds) *The Handicapped Person in the Community*. London: Tavistock, in association with The Open University.

Kersner, M. and Wright, J. (1996) *How to Manage Communication Problems in Young Children*. London: David Fulton Publishers.

Kiernan, C. and Kiernan, D. (1994) 'Challenging behaviour in schools for children with severe learning difficulties', *Mental Handicap Research* **7**, 117–201.

Kiernan, C. and Qureshi, H. (1993) 'Challenging behaviour', in Kiernan, C. (ed) *Research to Practice? Implications of Research on the Challenging Behaviour of People with Learning Disabilities*. London: British Institute of Learning Disabilities.

Lacey, P. (1998) ' Meeting needs through collaborative multidisciplinary teamwork', in Lacey, P. and Ouvry, C. (eds) *People with Profound and Multiple Learning Disabilities*. London: David Fulton Publishers.

Lacey, P. and Lomas, J. (1993) *Support Services and the Curriculum: A Practical Guide to Collaboration*. London: David Fulton Publishers.

Lancashire LEA (2000) *Performance Indicators for Value Added Target Setting*. Lancashire: Lancashire LEA.

Lawton, D. (1996) *Beyond the National Curriculum: Teacher Professionalism and Empowerment*. London: Hodder and Stoughton.

Locke, A. (1994) 'Speech and language difficulties', *Special Children* **72**, 21–5.

Locke, A. (1999) 'Why not teach the literacy hour?', *The SLD Experience* **24**, Summer, 2–4.

Longhorn, F. (2000) 'Numeracy for very special learners through host curricula and host environments', *The SLD Experience* **27**, Summer, 8–9.

McCaul, K. (2000) Curriculum development in a residential school for pupils with profound learning difficulties: an analysis of the processes and implications for multi-professional collaboration. Unpublished Ph.D. thesis. Oxford: Oxford Brookes University.

MacFarland, S. Z. C. (1995) *Journal of VI and Blindness* **89**, Part 3.

McInnes, J. M. and Treffry, J. A. (1982) *Deaf-Blind Infants and Children: A Developmental Guide*. Toronto: University of Toronto Press.

McNicholas, J. (2000) 'The assessment of pupils with profound and multiple learning difficulties', *British Journal of Special Education* **27**(3), 150–3.

Male, D. and May, D. (1997a) 'Stress, burnout and workload in teachers of children with severe learning difficulties', *British Journal of Special Education* **24**(3), 133–40.

Male, D. and May, D. (1997b) 'Burnout and workload in teachers of children with severe learning difficulties', *British Journal of Special Education* **25**(3), 117–21.

Marlett, N. (1984) *Program for the Severely and Profoundly Handicapped: The Last Educational Frontier*, unpublished manuscript, Special Educational Symposium, Winchester: King Alfred's College.

Marvin, C. (1994) 'Pupils with profound and multiple learning difficulties and the changing face of integration – an evaluation of a mainstream integration project'. Unpublished M Ed dissertation. Birmingham: School of Education, University of Birmingham.

Marvin, C. (1998) 'Teaching and learning for children with profound and multiple learning difficulties', in Lacey, P. and Ouvry, C. (eds) *People with Profound and Multiple Learning Disabilities*. London: David Fulton Publishers.

Mental Health Foundation (1997) *Don't Forget Us: Children With Learning Difficulties and Severe Challenging Behaviour*. London: Mental Health Foundation.

Morgan, J. *et al.* (1998) 'Strengthening the teaching team: teachers and paraprofessionals learning together', *Support for Learning* **13**(3), 115–17.

Morris, J. (1995) *Gone Missing? A Research and Policy Review of Disabled Children Living Away from their Families.* London: The Who Cares Trust.

National Curriculum Council (1992) *Curriculum Guidance 9: The National Curriculum and Pupils with Severe Learning Difficulties.* York: NCC.

Newman, D. W. and Beail, N. (1994) 'The assessment of need: a psychological perspective in people with learning disabilities', *Clinical Psychology Forum,* September, 21–5.

Nind, M. and Hewett, D. (1998) *Access to Communication.* London: David Fulton Publishers.

Norwich, B. (1990) 'How an entitlement can become a restraint', in Daniels, H. and Ware, J. (eds) *Special Educational Needs and the National Curriculum.* London: Kogan Page.

Norwich, B. (1996) 'Special needs education or education for all: connective specialisation and ideological impurity', *British Journal of Special Education* **23**,3, 100–4.

NUT (2000) *Advice, Guidance, Protection: Unacceptable Pupil Behaviour,* London: NUT.

OFSTED (1998) *Effective Action Planning After Inspection: Planning Improvement in Special Schools.* London: DfEE.

OFSTED (1999) *A Review of Special Schools, Secure Units and Pupil Referral Units in England.* London: The Stationery Office.

Oliver, M. (1996) *Understanding Disability from Theory to Practice.* Basingstoke: Macmillan.

Orelove, F. and Sobsey, D. (1993) *Educating Pupils with Multiple Disabilities, A Transdisciplinary Approach.* London: Paul Brookes.

Orr, R. (2000) 'Using sensory environments', *PMLD Link* **12**(2), 6–7.

Ouvry, C. (1987) 'Educating children with profound handicaps. Kidderminster: British Institute of Mental Handicap.

Ouvry, C. (1991) 'Access for pupils with profound and multiple learning difficulties', in Ashdown, R., Carpenter, B. and Bovair, K. (eds) *The Curriculum Challenge: Access to the National Curriculum for Pupils with Learning Difficulties.* London: Falmer Press.

Owens, P. (1997) *Early Childhood Education and Care.* London: Trentham.

Pagliano, P. (1999) *Multisensory Environments.* London: David Fulton Publishers.

Peter, M. (2000) 'Developing drama with children with autism', *Good Autism Practice* **1**(1), 9–20.

Pimm, P. (1998) 'Introduction to challenging behaviour', *British Journal of Occupational Therapy* **61**(7), 306–9.

Porter, J. (1986) 'Beyond a simple behavioural approach', in Coupe, J. and Porter, J. (eds) *The Education of Children with Severe Learning Difficulties.* London: Croom Helm.

Porter, J. (2000) 'The Importance of creating a mathematical environment', *The SLD Experience* **26**, Spring, 16–17.

Porter, J. and Miller, O. (2000) 'Developing the use of multisensory environments', *PMLD Link* **12**(2), 8–11.

Porter *et al.* (1997) *Curriculum Access for Deafblind Children: Research Report No 1.* DfEE

Powell, S. and Jordan, R. (1998) *Autism and Learning.* London: David Fulton Publishers.

Qualifications and Curriculum Authority (1999) *Shared World – Different Experiences: Designing the Curriculum for Pupils who are Deafblind.* London: QCA.

Qualifications and Curriculum Authority (2000a) *Personal, Social and Health Education at Key Stages 3 and 4.* London: QCA.

Qualifications and Curriculum Authority (2000b) *Citizenship at Key Stages 3 and 4.* London: QCA.

Robbins, B. (2000) 'Does teaching numeracy lead to mathematical learning?', *The SLD Experience* **26**, Spring, 9–12.

Roberts, V. Z. (1994) 'Conflict and collaboration: managing intergroup relations', in Obholzer, a. and Roberts, V. Z. (eds) *The Unconscious at Work.* London: Routledge.

Rose, R. (1991) 'A jigsaw approach to group work', *British Journal of Special Education* **18**(2), 54–7.

Rose, R., Fletcher, W. and Goodwin, G. (1999) 'Pupils with severe learning difficulties as personal target setters', *British Journal of Special Education* **26**(4), 206–12.

Rosen, S. (1997) 'Kinesiology and sensurimotor function', in Blasch, Wiener and Welsh (eds) *Foundations of Orientation and Mobility.* New York: American Foundation for the Blind.

Russell, P (1997) 'Access to the system: the legaslative interface' in Carpenter, B., Ashdown, R. and Bovair, K. (eds) *Enabling Access: Effective Teaching and Learning for Pupils with Learning Difficulties.* London: David Fulton Publishers.

Sanderson, H. *et al.* (1997) *People, Plans and Possibilities – Exploring People Centred Planning.* Edinburgh: Human Services Publications.

School Curriculum and Assessment Authority (1995) *Planning the Curriculum at Key Stages 1 and 2.* London: SCAA.

School Curriculum and Assessment Authority (1996a) *Assessment, Recording and Accreditation of Achievement for Pupils with Learning.* London: SCAA.

School Curriculum and Assessment Authority (1996b) *Planning the Curriculum for Pupils with Profound and Multiple Learning Difficulties.* London: SCAA.

School Curriculum and Assessment Authority (1997a) *Use of Language: A Common Approach.* London: SCAA.

School Curriculum and Assessment Authority (1997b) *Keeping the Curriculum under Review: Curriculum Planning and Development.* London: SCAA.

Sebba, J. and Rose, R. (1992) 'The National Curriculum: control or liberation for pupils with learning difficulties', *The Curriculum Journal* **3**(1), 143–60.

Sebba, J. *et al.* (1995) *Redefining the Whole Curriculum for Pupils with Learning Difficulties,* 2nd edn. London: David Fulton Publishers.

Sebba, J. *et al.* (1996) *Enhancing School Improvement through Inspection in Special Schools.* London: OFSTED.

Seligman, M. (1975) *Helplessness: On Depression, Development and Death.* San Francisco: Freeman.

Shon, D. (1983) *The Reflective Practitioner,* New York: Basic Books.

Smith, B. (1991) (ed.) *Interactive Approaches to Teaching the Core Subjects.* Bristol: Lame Duck Publishing.

Soder, M. (1992) 'Disability as a social construct', in Booth, T., Swann, W., Masterton, M. and Potts, P. (eds) *Policies for Diversity in Education.* London: Routledge.

Steers, R. M. and Porter, L.W. (1983) *Motivation and Work Behaviour.* New York: McGraw- Hill.

Styan, D. *et al.* (1990) *Developing School Management: The Way Forward* (report by the School Management Task Force) London: HMSO.

Sutherland, A. (1981) *Disabled we Stand.* London: Souvenir Press.

Tansley, A. E. and Gulliford, R. (1960) *The Education of Slow Learning Children.* London: Routledge Kegan Paul.

Teacher Training Agency (1999) *Effective Teachers of Numeracy.* Internet Service: www.teach-tta.gov.uk.

Thompson, D. and Barton, L (1992) 'The wider context: a free market', *British Journal of Special Education* **19**(1), 13–15.

Tilstone, C. (1996) 'Changing public attitudes', in Carpenter, B., Ashdown, R. and Bovair, K. (eds) *Enabling Access: Effective Teaching and Learning for Pupils with Learning Difficulties.* London: David Fulton Publishers.

Tilstone, C. *et al.* (2000) *Consultation Document: Curriculum Guidelines For Pupils Attaining Significantly Below Age-Related Expectations.* London: QCA/DfEE.

Turner, A. (2000) 'Redefining the past: OFSTED, SLD schools and the teaching of history', *British Journal of Special Education* **27**(2), 67–71.

United Nations (1989) *The Convention of the Rights of the Child.* New York: UN.

University of Durham (1999) *The P Levels Project.* Durham: University of Durham.

Valachou, A. (1997) *Struggles for Inclusive Education.* Buckingham: Open University Press.

Ware, J. (1990) 'The National curriculum for pupils with severe learning difficulties', in Daniels, H. and Ware, J. (eds) *Special Educational Needs and the National Curriculum.* London: Kogan Page.

Ware, J. (1996) *Creating a Responsive Environment for People with Profound and Multiple Learning Difficulties.* London: David Fulton Publishers.

Ware, J. (1994) *Educating Children with Profound and Multiple Learning Difficulties.* London: David Fulton Publishers.

Ware, J. and Healey, I. (1994) 'Conceptualising progress in children with profound and multiple learning difficulties', in Ware, J. (ed) *Educating Children with Profound and Multiple Learning Difficulties.* London: David Fulton Publishers.

Warnock, M. (1978) *Special Educational Needs: Report of the Committee of Enquiry into the Education of Handicapped Children and Young People* (The Warnock Report). London: HMSO

Warren, D. (1994) *Blindness and Children: An Individual Differences Approach.* Cambridge: Cambridge University Press.

West, M. and Ainscow, M. (1991) *Managing School Development: A Practical Guide.* London: David Fulton Publishers.

White, D. (1995) 'So now it's up to you', *Language and Learning,* March/April, 2.

Wing, L. (1996) *The Autistic Spectrum.* London: Constable.

Wright, J. and Kersner, M. (1998) *Supporting Children with Communication Problems.* London: David Fulton Publishers.

Index